BATTLEFIELD JAFFNA

BATTLEFIELD JAFFNA

ABANDONED, THEY FOUGHT...

Col Sunil Kotnala

Vitasta

Every soldier is willing to die
for his country,
just don't get him killed.

To my father,
Colonel Jagdamba Prasad Kotnala,
The finest soldier I have known.

Published by
Renu Kaul Verma
Vitasta Publishing Pvt Ltd
2/15, Ansari Road, Daryaganj
New Delhi – 110 002
info@vitastapublishing.com

ISBN 978-93-90961-48-1

First Edition 2023
MRP ₹495

Edited by Anuradha Mukherjee
Cover and layout by Somesh Kumar Mishra
Printed by Vikas Computer and Printers

CONTENTS

FOREWORD

The LTTE in Sri Lanka was the deadliest, most brutal separatist group the world had ever seen. It was not until the IPKF landed in Sri Lanka and the peace accord was thrown to the winds, that the Indian Army understood the impact of fighting insurgency on foreign soil. India had had its own insurgencies and militancy over the years, spread from the northeastern states of Manipur, Nagaland, and Mizoram, to recently in the northern state of Punjab, but had never confronted anything of the sort that awaited them in Sri Lanka. Being the third largest conventional army in the world, it seemed a foreign holiday to visit the island and implement a peace accord. The separatist groups were all India's creation, and the R&AW fully controlled them. But

Prabhakaran had different plans for them. Betrayed right from the beginning, he knew that he was just a pawn in the hands of the politicians on both sides of the Palk Strait.

Of course, in hindsight, it is easy to find faults and easy solutions, but the people involved at that time took decisions that they thought were correct. Unfortunately, these decisions cost many lives.

The Jaffna University Operation was a precursor to the Capture of Jaffna; both operations were launched without following the basics. The first one failed miserably and the second one cost many lives.

This book by Col Sunil Kotnala has been well researched and written in language that will make interesting reading even for non-military readers.

I am sanguine that these acts of heroism, courage, and brotherhood will instill a sense of pride and honour among the younger generation.

Jai Hind.

INTRODUCTION

Some called it 'India's Vietnam', and some said it was a strategic mistake directed by incompetent generals. There has been a lot of debate over the years about India's Vietnam and I am sure a few readers might not agree with my perspective on the issue.

With all humility and modesty, we must agree to disagree.

Military operations other than war (MOOTW) focus on deterring wars, resolving conflicts, promoting peace, and supporting civil authorities in response to domestic crises.

Every country that has undertaken such intervention missions or MOOTW has had its own 'Vietnam', and so did we. The USA in Vietnam against the Vietcong or in Somalia against the Somali warlord Mohamed Farrah Aidid and his Habar Gidir clan (remember Black Hawk Down), or Russia against the Talibanis are historical examples of repeated failures of superpowers in alien lands, for obvious reasons.

We had it too, fighting on alien land against alien people, for an alien cause. It was not a classical intervention because the GoSL had requested and invited India's help to resolve the Tamil crisis in their country. Unfortunately, it turned out to be a kind of war for which we were neither trained, equipped, nor had any experience. We were not psychologically prepared for its intensity, ruthlessness, and hostility. We were inducted with no clarity on the mission, on the use of lethal force, or even on who was friend or foe. The fog of war was thick and kept getting denser as the conflict progressed. With no political direction of the war, the army top brass used only fancy military jargon that was eventually converted into body bags.

To quote Shyam Tekwani, the only photographer to have been in the thick of it,

> 'In their shorts or lungis, with beardless faces and bare feet, they look like anything but battle-hardened guerrillas who have taken on the might of the fourth largest army in the world. Many are

> barely in their teens, some are young women, and no one looks a day older than thirty.
>
> Yet, the lethal weaponry they wield with such proficiency, the revolutionary zeal in their eyes, their intimate knowledge of the local terrain, and their absolute disdain for death describe how they have managed to give the 20,000-strong IPKF such a run for its money.'

But Operation Pawan, as the IPKF's operation in Sri Lanka was code-named, is a chapter of Indian military history that will contain none of the honour and glory of a victorious campaign, although it will have individual actions of grit and raw courage. Notwithstanding the fact that the IPKF fought against daunting odds and under severe constraints, the *liberation* of Jaffna was essentially an ego-satisfying operation.

For the first time, the Indian Army was inducted to fight in built-up areas (FIBUA), confronted with Improvised Explosive Devices (IEDs), multiple ambushes, suicide bombers, and cyanide ampules. Our enemy neither wore uniforms nor did they follow any of the ethics of war. We learnt our lessons the hard way, losing many young officers and soldiers. In the thirty-two-month deployment on the island, we lost a 1200 officers and men, and another

1000 were maimed and scarred for life. It was a catch-22 situation; the LTTE fighters who were friends until the night before, turned foe with all their might and fury, even before we realised what hit us. They killed, maimed, ambushed, kidnapped, and tortured the IPKF with impunity. The pleas to use our complete combat inventory and potential were denied by the politicians urging the IPKF to use minimum force so that the Indian doctrine of 'Ahimsa' did not take a beating. While our adversary was using modern weapons and communication equipment, we still used the vintage arsenal of WWII, and only the small arms at that. We were caught in a political quagmire.

To quote from the author's preface of the excellently researched and well-written book, *The Broken Palmyrah*,

> 'The collection of articles contained in these two volumes was written by us mostly in the three months following November 1987. This period marked the immediate aftermath of the Indian Army's October offensive that had the stated purpose of disarming the Tamil Tigers (or the Liberation Tigers of Tamil Eelam, the L.T.T.E.). The tragic results of this war came as a surprise to most Tamils who had just experienced two months of unprecedented peace. They expected no good from the Sri Lankan forces. From the militants,

> they had expected little more than to keep the Sri Lankan forces at bay. But from India, they had expected much. To add to the effects of the process culminating in the Indian offensive, Tamil society found itself in a state of paralysis, both moral and intellectual. The ordinary civilian is now caught, a helpless pawn in a game played by a multitude of forces. People were being threatened, robbed, beaten, and sometimes even killed. There were few signs of a community response.
>
> Amidst all this, the various actors had much to hide as well as their own myths to propagate. All had acquired a vested interest in suppressing the truth.'

The political agenda was not in line with the military doctrine, that is, if we even had one. The R&AW kept telling us that the LTTE were 'Our Boys' and these skirmishes were the work of a few rogues who would be brought in line in a few days. The days went on for weeks and months and years until we finally pulled out of the island on 24 March 1990, trying to save face. It was not easy for the field commanders to motivate and convince the soldiers on the ground that we were not fighting to protect Mother India but trying to implement a peace accord. There was no patriotic cause to be fighting in Sri Lanka. But still, the soldiers fought with all they had, which was raw courage, camaraderie, and regimentation.

The national and international media was against us and wrote whatever the LTTE propaganda machinery in Sri Lanka and the western countries fed them. Our reporters on the ground, who were few and far spread, picked up titbits of stories from everywhere and wrote epilogues far removed from the reality on the ground.

Human rights groups were left crying hoarse about mass scale rapes, genocide, and looting by the IPKF, most of it being fed by the influential Tamilian LTTE propaganda machinery based in Europe and the USA.

To top it all off, we were hounded by our own people who shared their ethnicity with the Sri Lankan Tamils. Sadly, the concept of India as a nation and 'being Indian' ceased when caste, creed, colour, and religion came to the forefront. In Chennai, where we generally reported while being inducted/de-inducted by sea or air route into Sri Lanka, the locals ill-treated the soldiers, taunting and heckling them. As if the happenings in Sri Lanka were not enough to scar our psyche, we also had to face the ire of the Tamilians in India. The hostility of the locals in Sri Lanka was understandable, but in India, it was heart breaking. They were not to be blamed really. The politicians had them by the tail and were fuelling anti-IPKF sentiments from their voter bases and the Tamilians abroad while keeping an eye on the upcoming elections.

Unlike the US Army, whose soldiers suffered from post-traumatic stress disorder (PTSD), the Indian soldier was never considered to have suffered any kind of post-conflict trauma. Sadly, with no such concept in the Indian Army, thousands (there were seventy-thousand troops at one time in Sri Lanka) of soldiers still carry psychological scars.

For the soldier, any conflict means fighting. So, he fights with all that he has, with the aim to win the battle he is in. Some succeed, some do not. Those who do succeed deserve to be applauded and awarded but those who fail do not deserve to be forgotten. Even in failed battles, the soldiers fought bravely and courageously, although the odds were seriously stacked against them. They lost due to no fault of theirs.

Sri Lanka had many such battles where the best of the best had to face defeat, not because they lacked military skills, but because they were inducted into battle with poor or no intelligence about the LTTE fighters, and military planning at the higher level was abysmal, to say the least. The initial days of the IPKF in Sri Lanka, when the peace accord fell apart, were the toughest. Gradually, with time, the officers and soldiers learnt their lessons the hard way and adapted tactics to use terrain and situations to effectively counter the LTTE fighters. They also learnt when not to follow directions from higher authorities.

It is a well-known fact that the peace accord between India and Sri Lanka was a still-born baby. It had failed the moment it was signed. Jayewardene was a shrewd and highly skilled politician compared to Rajiv Gandhi, who was a novice. The LTTE referred to them as 'Old Fox' and 'Cub Fox' respectively, which was based on their personalities. Although India had literally arm-twisted Sri Lanka to sign the accord by air-dropping food and medical aid during *Operation Eagle*, Jayewardene, the Old Fox that he was, ensured that the IPKF took the complete brunt of the LTTE head-on.

A lot has also been said and written against Major General Harkirat Singh, on his unprofessional approach and inept handling of the situation. I might not have the authority to comment on this, but the fact remains that commanders at all levels must accept both the bouquets and brickbats of their command. What is also true, is that there was a 'paradigm operational shift' which took some time to be absorbed by the senior and junior commanders alike.

The chain of command was established so that he had to wait for all his orders from Delhi, which either never came or came too late, from people who had no understanding of ground zero. To add to his misery, Maj Gen Harkirat Singh, GOC 54 Infantry Division (The IPKF Division in Sri Lanka), and Mr J.N. Dixit, the Indian High Commissioner in Sri Lanka, were not on the best of terms, which was a well-known fact. Unlike the civil services, the army hierarchy is completely based on merit and there is no assured career progression. Therefore, the fact that Maj Gen Harkirat Singh rose to the level of a Major General, speaks about his professional competence. Dixit often overstepped his charter of duty and passed direct orders to the General, which he rightly refused. The fact that Dixit tended to be high-handed and overbearing was because he had close ties with the Gandhi family and was Rajiv Gandhi's man in Colombo.

Maj Gen Harkirat Singh was finally made the fall guy, and all the others higher up on the chain of command absolved themselves of the failures in Sri Lanka. Again, the battalion commanders were the officers who got the boot, whether in terms of career advancement or awards and honours. Only a few commanding officers were awarded for gallantry despite being killed in operations, which is evidence enough that the commanders on the ground were made responsible in the failed operations for the capture of Jaffna.

I have not dwelled on the genesis of the Sri Lankan

problem as that makes for a separate reading and is a subject to be handled by historians. It suffices to say that ethnic problems anywhere in the world have deep roots in history and are too complicated to be sorted out by foreigners or foreign armies, no matter how good their intentions are.

Keeping in mind the strategic considerations like the intelligence inputs of foreign secret services, or intelligence agencies—including mercenary companies and especially Pakistan's ISI clandestinely at work in Sri Lanka—the Indian Government realised the gravity of the situation and sat up. Internal pressure from Tamilian groups to intervene in Sri Lanka to save the Tamils, citing the example of India's intervention in Bangladesh in 1971, was something the Rajiv Gandhi government could not wish away. Tamil Nadu is an important state in India and with sixty million Tamils in the country, there was no way the government could have pacified them without taking action equivalent to the intervention in Bangladesh. It is also on record that India was formally invited by the government of Sri Lanka, to assist them militarily when the Sri Lankan Armed Forces were to be moved from the Jaffna province, to quell the widespread JVP-organised riots in Colombo. The President of Sri Lanka had requested Rajiv Gandhi to send in some Indian troops to Jaffna and Trincomalee to fill in the vacuum that would be created.

This story is *not* a historical record of what happened with an infantry unit that was thrown in front of the Tiger (LTTE) with an assurance that he had been tamed by the trainers aka R&AW. It is in the public domain that the R&AW were training and arming the LTTE, the Eelam People's Revolutionary Liberation Front (EPRLF), the Eelam Revolutionary Organisation of Students (EROS), etc. since 1977. The then director of R&AW, Mr Anand Verma, is known to have categorically and candidly told Rajiv Gandhi that 'These are our boys, once they have agreed (to surrender arms) they will not betray'. So we went in thinking that the Tiger had no teeth and no claws; we just needed to put the leash around its neck and get him home. Sadly, the stakeholders in this complete campaign—politicians, diplomats, bureaucrats, intelligence agencies, and the military hierarchy were in for a big surprise when they went against the Tiger.

I have made an earnest effort to put this mission in the correct perspective, by going through whatever documents I could lay my hands on and meeting the officers and soldiers involved in the operation. It has taken me five years to produce this book, which is a reconstruction of the operation by the officers and soldiers involved, and eyewitness accounts.

Every soldier has his own perspective of an operation

depending on where and how he was placed at that point in time. Nonetheless, the story is one of the most poignant ever told and heard. It is my attempt to separate facts from imagination. I have relied on the integrity and credibility of the people who were involved in the operation. It is well known and documented that those in charge said what was convenient or acceptable to the people in power, and not what was right. Amazingly, each one of them remembers every minute detail of the operation.

The Jaffna University Special Heliborne Operations (SHBO) was undertaken with an aim to end the LTTE resistance early, and as a matter of fact, with one crippling blow. Undue hurry in launching the operation without adequate preparation, being blinded by ambition, and underestimating the enemy were the cardinal sins committed by our commanders, which resulted in the loss of precious lives and ultimately the failure of the operation. I have dwelled mainly on this operation in the book.

Furthermore, as per senior commanders in Delhi, the entire operation for the capture of Jaffna was supposed to take just three days. Instead, the mission turned into a nightmare, taking almost thirteen days to complete without breaking the LTTE's armed struggle. Prabhakaran, the LTTE supremo, and his trusted lieutenants still escaped capture. His complete cadre managed to escape out of Jaffna and took refuge in the jungles of Vavuniya and Trincomalee to fight another day, a classic guerrilla warfare tactic.

The Heliborne Operation at Jaffna University was the precursor to the capture of Jaffna. Unfortunately, it started disastrously. The situation in Sri Lanka, and more specifically in the Jaffna peninsula, spiralled out of control. It took years to finally realise that it was not our cup of tea and the earlier we got out of this mess the better it would be for us.

As a soldier and a writer, I was moved by the fact that in an operation where forty soldiers, twenty-nine from 13 Sikh LI and eleven from 10 Para Commando, were killed, had never been discussed or taught in any military school of instruction. A few articles have been written about it but often without much research and probing. Even the movie, *Madras Café*, dwells on it for only a few seconds. It hovers like a bad memory that everyone just wants to forget. Of course, 13 Sikh LI holds an *Ardas* every year on October 12, to commemorate this momentous day.

This SHBO was launched on the night of 11 October 1987, woefully lacking basic military practices. What happened on that night? How could a superior army suffer such losses? How was a highly motivated task force comprising of the Sikh Light Infantry and the Para

Commandoes undone by a group of rag-tag revolutionaries? Where was the failure? What were the soldiers thinking when they knew that there was no way out from here? Did they know they would be killed? Except for Sepoy Gora Singh of 13 Sikh LI, no one survived the ill-fated operation from his team to give me the answers I searched for. Unfortunately, as a young and inexperienced soldier, he did not have much to add to my research. All these questions have haunted me for many years. I, as an officer, can feel the helplessness and frustration of the officers of 13 Sikh LI and 10 Para Commando who were leading this mission, aware that no help was coming.

The 13th Battalion of the Sikh Light Infantry Regiment, 'Guru's Own', as it is known, had been in Bangalore for two months, ready to be inducted into Sri Lanka. With orders to return to their base at Gwalior, they were again airlifted to Vavuniya and Trincomalee in Sri Lanka. At Tambaram, where they halted for refuelling the aircraft, they were diverted to Palaly and launched into an SHBO immediately, along with a company of the 10th Battalion, The Parachute Regiment (Commando), that had been stationed at Palaly since July 1987.

Unknown terrain, complacency, faulty intelligence and planning, inadequate briefing, understrength, non-coordination, and total lack of preparation time proved disastrous for the soldiers of both the units, who were air-dropped into Jaffna University.

Further knee-jerk reactions and the lack of major tactical flexibility and contingency planning against a determined and well-fortified enemy multiplied the confusion and chaos among the ground troops, who tried helplessly to link up with the air-dropped team by road. What transpired at various stages of the operation by way of time, locations, and actual operations is what I have attempted to chronologize in this book. I do not claim that every paragraph, sentence, and word is 'as it happened', but I do claim that my intentions, the incidents as told by various participants of the operation, and whatever is in the public domain are true to the last word. I have taken liberties in certain places to weave it into a readable and interesting novel so that it does become akin to a historical record. Incidents involving persons who are no more amidst us have been reconstructed with available facts, keeping in mind all sensitivities and respect that is due to these soldiers killed in action. The attempt is that it must make interesting reading to the non-military readership so that they can see beyond the spit and polish of the army. That is all.

This is the story of the 13th Battalion of the Sikh LI Regiment and their saga in Sri Lanka between 10 October and 24 October 1987 (although they stayed for a longer period). From being caught off guard in the initial stages of the operation, the unit transformed overnight into a well-oiled fighting machine. The depleted strength of personnel was compensated for by the teachings of brotherhood given by the Sikh Gurus. The outstanding leadership of the officers and JCOs who led from the front overcoming all the challenges that came their way was commendable. With total faith in their Commanding Officer to lead them and in the men to follow them, they uprooted the LTTE fighters from their well-entrenched positions one after the other in a short time frame. Let me assure the readers that doing this in an alien land with no maps, guides, air cover, or artillery fire support, coupled with a heavy downpour of torrential rain, is an arduous task that is difficult even for military commanders to fathom unless they have been amidst it.

Within just four or five hours of their arrival in Sri Lanka, the unit went through a baptism by fire. In the first seventy-two hours, they suffered about forty fatal casualties, and until the capture of Jaffna, the unit had lost a total of sixty-two officers and men, with another fifty injured. For a Commanding Officer who treated his officers and men like his children, this was cause for lifelong trauma. Even today, he cannot narrate a single incident of that fateful night without weeping his heart out.

The street smartness, superior training, and operational experience of the 10th Battalion of the Parachute Regiment (Commando) saved the day and was a lesson for all conventional military outfits. Outnumbered, surrounded, and cornered they fought for thirty-two hours, with their backs literally against the walls of three houses. Although a Commando unit, they were equipped with weapons similar to an Infantry unit. The fact that they had trained to operate in small teams and that the junior leadership lived up to the occasion, gave them the capability and tactical independence to manoeuvre to advantageous positions. They had unknowingly entered the LTTE HQ and were outnumbered at least 1:5, with the LTTE fighters pouring in from neighbouring villages. Had it not been for their Commanding Officer with his team, who linked up with them at the nick of time with a troop of tanks, the story would have been bloodily different. There are very few historical examples of such grit, unflinching loyalty, and supreme confidence in training anywhere in military history.

Every Air Force pilot, whether helicopter or fighter, believes that the ultimate test of his flying skills is on the battlefield—no Ray-Bans, no swagger, just him and his machine. Like any other soldier, his true character will be seen in all its nakedness when the bullets fly. The five MI8 helicopters used in this operation had been flown in from different air force bases in India. Until this day, they mostly had administrative duties and/or ferried the fighters of Tamil Eelam. That night changed every perspective that any of the pilots had about 'real combat'. They flew at night without any day reconnaissance of the dropping zone, and of course, no maps. They made consecutive landings even when effective fire rained on them from every possible direction. Even when the helicopters were damaged, they kept ferrying the soldiers until they could not fly anymore. It was a miracle the helicopters could fly back after the last sortie. As if this was not enough, they had to face an inquiry after the dust settled down. Compare this with the UNSOM-II mission in Mogadishu, Somalia, aka Black Hawk Down, where two UH-60 Black Hawk helicopters were shot down. Despite the highly sophisticated technology and weapons at their disposal, the elite forces of the US army lost nineteen soldiers with seventy-three injured.

Unfortunately, as it often happens, the soldiers who fight are seldom recognised for their deeds and the ones who botch up operations further are rewarded by getting plum appointments. The incompetent favours the incompetent or 'mango begets mango'. It is unsurprising then, that nothing happened to the seniors who should have been held responsible for the loss of lives. Everyone higher up in the line got what they did not deserve. That is how the world rotates.

I am indebted to all officers and soldiers who candidly shared their personal traumatic experiences and helped me in researching and writing this book. Without their guidance, I would have been left groping in the dark. My special thanks to the Sri Lanka veterans, Lt Gen Depinder Singh, GOC-in-C Southern Command and Overall Commander IPKF, as well as Maj Gen Sheonan Singh and Col RS. Bhadouriya, both 10th Battalion of the Parachute Regiment (Commando). To Maj Gen Hoshiyar Singh, Col GS, HQ 54 Inf Div; Col RS Sethi, CO, 13 Sikh LI; Col Shivalkar; Col CB Sharma, 13 Sikh LI; Air Commodore Sapre; and V Prakash.

I write this book to commemorate and honour those brave souls who fought against all odds with sheer raw courage, nerves of steel, camaraderie, and esprit de corps to lay down their lives, upholding the greatest tradition of being a soldier.

JAI HIND

PRELUDE: CDO RAID

1980

The first of the three MI8 helicopters flew into the designated drop zone (DZ), its down draft kicking up dust on its way, the vegetation fluttering as if in acknowledgement of its arrival. Lieutenant Birender 'Biru' Singh noticed that the fog had nearly cleared off now. They were lucky to get a two-hour window of clear weather. This year, the entire area had been experiencing freak weather. The night temperatures over the last week had plummeted to below 7°C, and a dense fog had descended over the entire district. The flight commander had confirmed late in the evening, that he had received the 'Go Ahead' as the MET team had seen favourable weather within the 'minima' in their report to him. They were lucky to have this window, Biru thought, otherwise, with 30 kgs on the back, the 20 kilometre trudge on hostile terrain would have been a killer. The militants were no less hostile than the weather and terrain. They were deadly fighters, and with the advantage of knowing the jungle like the back of their hand, they always had predominance while operating against the Indian Army.

Dispelling his thoughts, he looked at the Air Force sergeant to give him the legendary thumbs-up sign for the slithering to commence. The helicopter (heptr) was now hovering over the DZ. Lt Mukesh 'Mike' Singh was on the first rope and his buddy was on the one beside him. The time was 0030 hours IST. The Air Force sergeant was holding a lashing rope with his right hand, and with his left, the belt of the battle buddy. A red light near the sergeant's right hand on the helicopter panel flickered, 'Stand by', he shouted.

The red changed to green.

'Go, go', he shouted, trying to be heard over the deafening sound of the rotors as he removed his hand from his buddy's belt and patted him on his back.

Mike and his buddy vanished into the darkness below. The first buddy pair of the Pathfinders were on the ground, and then the next, until all seven buddy pairs hit the ground. They spread out in all the cardinal directions and took up defensive positions to receive the next wave of heptrs and commandoes.

Biru was the last to slither out of the heptr, with his buddy on the next rope. With the dense undergrowth at the DZ, the heptr was not kicking up any dust now, but the downdraft was enough to create air resistance and mild disorientation. The sergeant pulled up the ropes and gave an all-clear to the pilots. The heptr swerved to the west and left the helipad. The next one on its tail came in to repeat the same drill. Biru gave the torch signal to the pilot, indicating that the helipad had been secured. The heptr hovered, and the slithering commenced. Lt Arney 'Chits' Chitkara with his team, slithered and moved ahead of the pathfinders. He secured the area and reported all clear to Biru. Lt Devbrat 'Dev' Ohri confirmed the support party in the third area. Once they were all on the ground and Biru got the 'all okay' report from the three parties, they commenced their move towards the designated commando base.

Their mission was to raid and capture the top leadership of the deadliest, most ruthless, and heavily armed militant group operating in northeastern India. In the last few years, this militant group had acquired sophisticated arms and communication equipment from the neighbouring country. They had punitively attacked Indian Army convoys, patrols, and isolated camps in the jungles.

Recently, in a prominent town in Nagaland, they had laid a large ambush for a Commanding Officer's convoy. The army had suffered heavy fatal casualties, including the CO. It was this incident that really triggered the army to take decisive action against this particular militant group.

Thus, this commando raid was planned and was now being executed. Biru had thoroughly briefed and rehearsed with his team. Till now, the execution was as per the plan, and they had not encountered any militant interference. Complete radio silence was being maintained to avoid any intercepts by the militants. The team moved cautiously, following the navigation party that was leading the way. They had started ascending a feature that was heavily covered with undergrowth, and the vines between trees were slowing them down. Biru detailed another two buddy pairs to move ahead of the leading scouts, to cut their way through with dahs and khukris. Dev, who was now the navigation party commander, indicated a halt. The team took up positions all around, and Biru moved ahead. Dev whispered that they had reached the edge of the hill and that they were ascending. Both of them moved a little distance ahead, and then they could hear the angry wild roar and fury of the fast-flowing river, deep inside the gorge ahead of them. The river had cut through the mountain and formed a deep gorge, meandering its way downstream. The sound was deafening and overwhelming. It was pitch dark and fog had started to descend into the jungle. Biru knew that they had to move quickly before it would become difficult to negotiate the descent into the gorge.

Biru and Dev moved back to where the team was positioned. He called up Mike, and as per the plan told him to move ahead. Mike and his party quickly fixed four ropes on the tree trunks to descend into the gorge. With only the leading buddy pairs wearing night-vision goggles (NVGs), the others just followed, believing that they would reach the bottom of the gorge.

At the edge of the river, the sound was now absolutely deafening, and the spray of water drenched every single one of them to the bone. Their misery was further aggravated by the cold and the equipment's weight, which had become twice as heavy after getting wet. Biru sent out two reconnaissance parties along the river to look for a crossing place. There were none at least 500 metres in both directions, up and downstream. Dev did report some fallen trees lying at a location that could be developed into a crossing site with some effort.

The team moved upstream and started building a crossing point. With great difficulty and effort, two dried-up dragon fruit tree trunks, about 30 feet in length, were placed across. One wrong step meant being swept away by the monstrous river and facing certain death. Slowly and carefully, the team crossed over. Then began the long and treacherous climb up the gorge, through loose mud and boulders, the dense fog, cold and drenched equipment and uniforms making it harder. After a two-hour trek, the navigation party located the commando base they had planned on the map. As per orders, all heavy equipment was dropped there and the team, without much ado, left with arms, ammunition, and communication equipment required for the final phase of the mission. The time now was 0300 hours, just ninety minutes remaining to complete the task, after which it would be first light—the lurking danger of being daylighted and losing the surprise element.

The team began closing in on the target area, and Mike with his buddy and another buddy pair, crawled ahead towards the two militants who were callously guarding the western side of the camp, as though no animal or human would possibly take this approach to the militant base. The gorge with the fast-flowing river was a no go in the first place, and then the steep ascent on their side made it a suicidal approach, not intended to be taken by any group that intended to even reach the camp.

Mike, with his buddy, sneaked in close to the sentries, who were silenced even before they realised what happened. Mike gave the signal of all clear to Biru. Dev with his team had already taken up positions square of the assaulting team being led by Biru, and they deployed their automatic weapons. The support party would only come into play in case the surprise factor was lost, and they needed to extricate Biru and his team from the target area.

Capt Sheonan 'Sheonan' Singh at the headquarters operation control room was a worried man. There had been no communication with Biru's team since they had been inserted. The route was treacherous, and with the dense fog, he just prayed for everyone's safety. He should not have given the go-ahead for the mission, but Biru was insistent, and his plan seemed workable. The general sitting in front of the mission map board looked up at Sheonan, shaking his head in impatience.

The militant camp had been there for the last four years and was so well located in the interiors of the dense jungle, that its occupants never thought that the Indian Army would ever find them, let alone plan and execute an operation against them. Spread over a radius of 200 metres it had six bamboo huts lined up in a semi-circle with sentry posts on the periphery, which over time had been left unattended. The huts were constructed on stilts to protect them from the fast-flowing groundwater during monsoons. Each hut had a door facing the open area in front and two windows on both sides. The roofs were also made of bamboo and covered with dragon leaves. The area in front of the huts had been cleared of any vegetation and had bamboo benches and stools.

The raiding party under Biru had moved into the camp very stealthily, like shadows. Mike and his team placed explosives on the fuel barrels, ammunition dumps, and living huts. Biru's team was now running towards the group of three huts that housed the top leadership of the militant group. Biru hoped that the intelligence input about the layout of the camp was correct. His team was now divided into two parties. One laid the cordon around the huts, and the other, with three buddy pairs, kicked open the doors of the huts and entered. The self-styled Commander-in-Chief lay comfortably in his sleeping bag when he heard the door crash open.

Capt Sheonan and General Aditya 'Ad' Verma were still in front of the map board when their door banged open.

'What the fuck is this?', Ad said, jumping hastily from his chair.

He turned around, as did Sheonan.

Biru saluted.

'Codeword Lal Badshah, Sir', he said.

'Where the fuck have you come in from, Biru?', the general asked, rather surprised on seeing him.

Biru smiled and looked at Sheonan.

Sheonan picked up the handset of the radio set.

'All stations, codeword Lal Badshah, I repeat, codeword Lal Badshah, Over', indicating freezing of the exercise.

After forty-three days of gruelling, rigorous, and sometimes nearly inhumane training, the commando course had finally culminated in this grand finale—Exercise Vijay. Biru and his team had caught the 'exercise enemy' and had taken the staff completely by surprise. No one had expected the raiding party to take the approach from the gorge. It was a suicidal route and had never been attempted by the previous 102 commando courses, but this 103 course had attempted it successfully. Sheonan was genuinely pleased with the conduct of the raid, and especially with the surprise factor that they had achieved.

Gen Ad was furious. He had not been told the route that the team would be taking, thereby saving themselves from being denied of its use.

'Why was this route taken by this team, when as per training policy it is not allowed? I think Biru has been reckless and immature by putting the lives of so many trainee officers at risk', he said to Sheonan, who was the directing staff for this exercise.

Before he could reply, Ad continued, 'I want an inquiry to be conducted and strict disciplinary action taken against Lt Birender Singh, is that understood?'

'Sir, the boy has thought out-of-the-box', argued Sheonan, 'And thinking out-of-the-box and executing a raid with this kind of finesse is the essence of the training and a successful commando raid', he continued.

'Don't you give me the essence and finesse story, my dear. In all exercises, certain parameters and protocols have to be adhered to', he shouted.

'I agree Sir, but…'

It took some time, and a hard stand by Capt Sheonan, to finally convince Ad, who was initially not ready to listen to any such arguments. Somehow Sheonan prevailed, and the case was decided in favour of Biru.

This got him the 'Best Student' and the 'Commando Dagger' award on the course. During the break-off party at the Commando School later in the evening the next day, Sheonan walked up to Biru and said, 'Biru, I saved you this time, but I may not be able to do so next time.' Both of them laughed.

THE SRI LANKA PEACE ACCORD - IN TATTERS

CHAPTER 1

THE START

It was a clear third October afternoon, the sea breeze blew steadily from the west to the east, across the deck of the blue and white marine fishing craft crossing the serene emerald green waters of the Indian Ocean. The lone boat seemed to be at peace with itself. Smoothly and soundlessly, it rocked like a child in a cradle and floated effortlessly in a forward motion, cutting the water as it moved ahead.

During the entire journey, from Koddikarai in Tamil Nadu where the boat had set sail, the fourteen LTTE men (Liberation Tigers of Tamil Eelam) on board had been crammed on the lower deck of the boat. Now that they were in international waters and away from the Indian Coast Guards, they had nothing to fear. They had come up to the upper deck and were basking in the sun. They were all returning to Jaffna, bringing along with them a huge cache of arms and other warlike stores, supplied to them by the R&AW (Research & Analysis Wing). The Indo-Sri Lanka accord did not allow any movement of warlike stores in or out of Sri Lanka. The coverup story was obviously that they were shifting their office stores from Rameshwaram to the island. They had set sail from the fishing port town of Koddikarai, which was known for smuggling bidis for opium, and was now infamous for the landing of illicit arms for the LTTE. The smuggling of arms and ammunition had been going on for many years, and the whole illegal apparatus involved in this operation functioned like well-oiled machinery.

There had been an impasse over the implementation of the constitution of the interim administration council for the development of Jaffna after the Sri Lanka-India peace accord had been signed. The senior members of the government in Colombo were trying their best to sabotage the Sri Lanka-India Peace Accord. There were whispers in the corridors of power, that the SLAF (Sri Lankan Armed Forces) may stage a coup to overthrow the democratically elected government. The JVP, a prominent Sinhalese political party, was dead against the accord too, and the LTTE Supremo, Prabhakaran, had agreed to be a party to the accord, albeit unwillingly.

With the implementation of the accord still in a quandary, this was a good time, thought Pulendran, the Batticoloa LTTE Commander, to clandestinely smuggle some weapons from India to Sri Lanka to further arm his cadres in Batticoloa and Trincomalee. Prabhakaran had been urging him for some time now, to collect all the weapons lying in their Indian office at Rameshwaram, along with everything the R&AW had promised them. He was wary of the intentions of the Indian government, who he thought would withdraw their support whenever the heat shifted onto them. But his fears were laid to rest for the time being, when the R&AW agreed to give them a huge cache of arms, thereby keeping their word. He had sent Pulendran and Kumarappa, the Trincomalee LTTE commander and also his brother-in-law, to get the weapons. They were both self-styled Lieutenant Colonels in the LTTE Army. As the IPKF presence in the Jaffna Peninsula was increasing in number, Prabhakaran thought that they needed to be prepared for any eventuality.

Rameshwaram, a small town geographically closest to the northern territory of Sri Lanka, was the stronghold of the LTTE. For operational and administrative ease, this town suited the LTTE. They had tremendous support for their cause of the Tamil Eelam among the Tamils in India. Unlike in Sri Lanka, the police were not hostile here and they could hold demonstrations and public rallies to propagate their agenda, openly criticising the government and its agencies hounding them in Sri Lanka. It was also simpler and easier to get their weapons and other warlike stores from the Indian clandestine organisations supporting them in this war of liberation. The Tamil Nadu politicians openly supported them, both morally and financially. The hospitals were open for them to get their sick and wounded treated. Even the local population welcomed them with open arms.

'Kumar, how many weapons did we finally load on the boat?', Pulendran shouted and asked.

'Ananda, how many?', Kumar asked his second-in-command. Lt (SS) Anandakumar was a meticulous man. He pulled out a small paper from his pocket and read out of it, 'Hmm… fifty-four AK-47s, eight RPGs, seven SLRs…'

'Okay okay, that is a whole lot of stuff. Kumar lets divide them fifty-fifty between Trinco and Batticoloa. Is that okay with you?', Pulendran asked.

'Yeah, I think so, for the time being, it is okay. I have also asked Kittu to get in touch with the R&AW station commander in Madras and send us some more weapons and explosives. The R&AW may drop them in Jaffna in a day or two', he added.

The monotony of sea travel and the rhythmic rocking

of the boat made it difficult for Pulendran to keep his eyes open. He was drifting in and out of sleep.

This fishing boat had been loaned to them by Mr Ravi Iyer, who controlled the private fishing industry in Tamil Nadu. Mr Iyer was a sympathiser of the LTTE and their ideology. He was also an active member of the ruling MGR-led DMK party, and as a loyal party soldier, he followed orders without questioning them.

The boat was a stern trawler and was a common fishing boat used in Tamil Nadu. Stern trawling was the most widespread method of fishing in India. The vessel was 40 feet in length and was fitted with a 120 horsepower engine, although it had been switched off now because the waves were assisting them in moving forward, and they wanted to enter the port Point Pedro Lagoon late in the afternoon. This would facilitate hiding both their entry into the lagoon and ferrying the weapons inland.

The boat had two levels. The one underneath the deck had adequate storage space to hide the weapons. There were four sleeping bunks, a small pantry, and some space to stock foodstuff. This is where the men were hiding when they moved out of Rameshwaram. They had started early in the morning to avoid the coast guard. The ETA at Point Pedro was three o'clock; another hour to go. Kumar also lay down on the deck next to Pulendran, hoping to catch up on some sleep since he had not slept a wink in the last forty-eight hours.

The R&AW, as a practice, would always delay the supply of arms and ammunition. This was done to verify the authenticity of the party that had come to collect the stores, checking and rechecking to ensure that they would not fall into the hands of unknown or rival groups. It was difficult to distinguish one LTTE operative from the other, and therefore it took some time to establish their identity. All this had taken forty-eight hours, and then the shifting of the delivery location had further added to the lack of rest for Kumar, who was responsible for the collection.

The port of Point Pedro still had pockets that were dominated by the LTTE, and therefore was a safer landing ground for them. The LTTE cadres at the port would then ferry the cache of arms and explosives into the hinterland—Vavuniya and Trincomalee—along the well-guarded highways under their control.

Pulendran opened his eyes, squinting in the bright afternoon sun, and smiled at Kumar. Their camaraderie went back many years. They were the pioneers of the LTTE's armed confrontation with the GOSL. Prabhakaran was initially a wee bit sceptical about an armed conflict, but he listened to his lieutenants and also to the assurance given by the Indian government, and after tasting the initial success against the SLAF, he was in it, hook, line, and sinker.

'You think the IPKF will ditch us when the shit hits the fan?', Kumar asked Pulendran.

'Even before that', he replied.

'Why do you say that?', Kumar asked.

'You know that Jayewardene has been forced to sign the accord after India forcibly dropped medical and food supplies for us in Jaffna on the fourth of June, during Operation Poomalai, or Operation Eagle 4, as they called it. They literally had the gun to his head, and Thamby (as Prabhakaran was known among his senior cadres) wasn't even made a party to it, although they had promised to read out the draft to him. They kept him in Delhi when the accord was signed. So really, the only interested party is India, for whatever strategic gains they may accrue out of the accord. We are not Bangladesh. Here, the stakes are different, and they may support us only until MGR has relevance in the Rajiv Gandhi government. You and I know that Jayewardene, the "Old Fox", is a shrewd and seasoned politician, and as compared to him, Rajiv Gandhi is a kindergarten toddler, a "Cub Fox". He has made sure that the onus of implementation of the peace accord lies with India, so finally, he is going to get two friends, us and India, involved in a fight against each other without either of us knowing about it. Mark my words', Pulendran replied, rather scholarly.

'So what will Jayewardene do now?', Kumar probed further.

'Well, I think he will create a situation where the IPKF will be forced to fight with all its might against us. That way, all the blame shifts to the IPKF, and Jayewardene gets what he wants', he said, concluding his argument.

'Navy boat, navy boat!', shouted the lookout man.

Kumar whipped out his binoculars and looked through them. The lookout man, for once, was correct. The Sri Lankan Navy vessel was heading towards them using their signal lights to indicate something to them. Kumar was a trained mariner and deciphered the codes.

'They want us to stop and identify ourselves', he told Pulendran.

'Not now, we are north of Valvettithurai and about to reach Point Pedro', he instructed Kumar.

'They may open fire. They are heavily armed', said Kumar.

'No, they will not. After the peace accord, they do not have the mandate. They cannot even arrest us, it will work against them. And if they do, we can tell the international media that we have been harassed by the Sri Lankan Military. Do not worry. Just tell them to follow us',

Pulendran replied calmly. He was still lying on his back on the deck, with his left eye half-open in a squint.

Kumar liked him for his fearlessness and cool-headedness. He would be the most appropriate replacement for Thamby whenever the time comes, he thought.

The Sri Lankan Navy boat was closer to them now, and Kumar shouted, 'Follow us.'

The Naval commander on the boat smiled and asked, 'Where to mate?' The others on his boat laughed at his false sense of bravado, knowing full well where they were headed, now just ten minutes from where they were.

'Point Pedro', replied Kumar.

'Okay, we are with you mate', the Commander said.

They were just a bend away from the Point Pedro harbour, and both the boats slowed down.

The Point Pedro harbour just about qualified being called a harbour. It was more of a small parking place for boats and no big merchant ship could really get in. It was mostly used by fishing and tourist boats. The latter, of course, had vanished since the civil war began in Sri Lanka. The place was known for its pristine beaches, clean blue water, and laid-back lifestyle that held a hint of the colonial era. For India, it was a strategic point closest to her southern tip, and mythologically, the Ram Setu once connected the two towns of Rameshwaram and Point Pedro.

Pulendran was surprised to see a large contingent of the Naval and Military police along with Special Forces of the SLAF at the harbour, along with the immigration officials. The LTTE cadres who were supposed to be at the port for their reception were palpably missing.

As their boat anchored, the immigration officials, along with a few military police soldiers got onto it and walked towards Pulendran.

'Who is the captain here?', asked a young captain.

'We all are captains', replied Pulendran sarcastically, undeterred by their presence.

'We need to see your papers', the captain said, avoiding confrontation and argument with him.

'What papers are you looking for Captain?'

Pulendran's body language and tone demonstrated a 'couldn't-care-less' attitude..

'Your travel documents, your authorisation to travel from India to Sri Lanka', the captain replied.

Things were getting serious, thought Kumar. He did not want this to go on any longer lest they uncover the weapons and explosives on the boat. That, once discovered by the military police, could get them into real trouble.

'We do not require documents to travel, Captain', replied Pulendran.

'Listen to me very carefully, if you are a Sri Lankan

citizen then you need travel documents, otherwise, it is illegal to travel. If you are not a Sri Lankan citizen, then you have illegally entered our country. In both cases, I shall arrest you and your accomplices. Is that understood?' The captain tone was harsher and business-like now.

'Ha, you do not have the mandate to arrest any one of us. Don't think I do not know what the implications of the peace accord are. All of you guys have to sit in your barracks and the IPKF will implement the accord. So, just get off our back and let us go', Pulendran said.

This was the last straw. The captain looked towards his detail standing behind him.

'Search the boat', he ordered.

'You have no right to search our boat', Pulendran shouted.

'I even have the right to open fire in self-defence. Do you understand that?', the captain replied, stressing on the word 'even'.

This shut Pulendran up. He understood that the captain knew the rules and meant every word he had just said. He also noticed him eagerly fiddling with the snap button on his 9mm pistol holster.

It was not long after that they found the weapons and the other stores in the deck below. They counted it all.

'So this is what you got from the Indians, to fight your

own countrymen. You are traitors and should be shot here and now. But unfortunately, the Indians have tricked us into this peace accord, which will only spell doom for our country. As far as you all are concerned, you will also not be spared by the IPKF, and mark my words, they will not spare you', spat the captain.

'Take them into custody', he ordered his detail.

'I am warning you again Captain, it is against the accord to arrest us', Pulendran retorted.

'You are carrying weapons and warlike stores, which is against the accord, and I am not arresting you, I am only taking you into custody. There is a subtle difference between the two in legal parlance', the captain answered, a smile of victory on his face.

'You may have to pay for this with your life', Pulendran threatened, firing the last arrow from his quiver.

'I may later, but you may have to do it on the way, when you try to escape from custody after snatching a weapon from my soldier.'

Pulendran got the hint. He had heard of many such false encounters perpetuated by the SLAF. He had also killed 126 bus passengers about a month ago and had passed it off using a similar story.

He knew that the captain was just waiting to find an excuse to eliminate them. This shut him up completely. He looked towards Kumar, gesturing to follow the instructions of the captain. Kumar's shoulders had already drooped and the rest of the LTTE operatives just followed suit.

The soldiers pushed them inside a military truck that had longitudinal seating on both sides—the port and the starboard side—and a tail board to close the rear opening. The upper body was covered with tarpaulin, about 5 feet high, tied to an iron frame. The driver's cabin was separate from the main body of the truck, joined at the chassis level, with the fuel tank in between. Pulendran recognised it as a Nissan 4W73, commonly known as the 1-ton truck, now being extensively used by the SLAF since the truck's rear frame could be dismantled and used as an open weapon platform. Since the number of LTTE ambushes and sniper incidents on the SLAF had increased, the latter had modified these trucks to increase their firepower and all-round observation abilities.

All the LTTE men bundled into the 1-ton had no handcuffs on. Kumar understood why this was done. The aim of the SLAF was to make the LTTE operatives complacent so they might attempt to escape, which would give them enough reason to shoot and kill. Kumar instructed his cadre not to even think of doing anything that could remotely hint that they were trying to escape.

'These guys will open fire to kill, they actually want

and are waiting for us to make an attempt', he said.

The captain sitting in the co-driver's seat was frustrated. He had orders not to eliminate these LTTE fighters under any circumstances. The GOSL wanted them alive, and that too at Colombo. Let military issues be sorted militarily, he thought.

The journey was just about forty minutes long. They passed through the crowded town of Karavoddi-Thandamanaru and hit the Jaffna-Poonalai-Point Pedro road. Pulendran felt safer in crowded towns; it would not be easy to eliminate them by staging a false encounter here. He knew the area like the back of his hand and understood where they were headed.

They turned west on the highway and headed toward their destination. The roads were deserted, except for a few military vehicles that drove in pairs.

'Why are you taking us to the Palaly airport?', Pulendran asked the soldier who was sitting across from him in the truck.

'Don't know, ask the captain', he replied.

The captain was sitting in the front seat of the truck. Pulendran moved ahead and opened the small window slit between them.

'Why are you taking us to the airport?', he asked the captain, shouting over the noise of the engine and the gushing wind.

'We will put you on a flight back to India', the captain laughed and replied. 'We will keep you in custody until we know who takes you, us or the IPKF.'

'That's better', Pulendran said and closed the window.

Somewhere on the way, they stopped and picked up another four LTTE fighters whom the SLAF had arrested from a village.

It was around five o'clock, when they entered the airport.

Palaly Airport: The Chaos begins

Flying officer V Prakash was in the makeshift officer mess in the airport's small arrival lounge, sitting with the other officers having their evening tea when Flight Commander Winco Sapre entered hurriedly.

'We need to clear this building immediately', he said, addressing all the officers.

'Why, Sir?', Prakash asked.

'The SLAF has some LTTE guys and they want to keep them here', he replied.

'And where do we go?', asked Squadron Leader Vinayraj.

'To the bungalow next door', Sapre replied with finality.

'No Sir, I mean the mess?', Prakash continued.

'We will decide that later, as of now, just clear off.'

They were all helicopter pilots and had moved into

Jaffna and the Palaly airport not too long ago. They got up and went into their rooms to pack up whatever meagre belonging they had carried with them from India during their induction.

Prakash had moved from Jodhpur and had recently converted as a pilot, from the Chetak helicopters to MI8s. He had expected his posting to move from Barielly, where he had been for two years, to somewhere in the Northeast, to gain more experience in flying the MI8s, but the Air Headquarters had instead posted him to Jodhpur.

He had nearly gone into depression after getting his posting orders, more so because his CO had assured him a posting of his choice. But the Air Headquarters had operational compulsions as they had always said.

During his farewell interview, his CO had said, 'Prakash, you never know what the future has in store for you. Maybe Jodhpur will prove to be a turning point in your career and life, just fly on.' Within a few months, these words turned out to be true.

In a few days, after landing at Jodhpur, he realised that he may never get a chance to captain a heptr. The unit he was in was overloaded with senior wing commanders who would not even let him hold the rudder. For two months, he flew as the co-pilot, just sitting and navigating for the captains. He cursed the moment he had joined the IAF and the moment he had been posted to Jodhpur.

Then, as there is spring after winter, one day, in August 1987, due to an upgrade of appointments in the Air Force, nearly all the wing commanders were posted outside, and he was, for the first time, allowed to captain a flight. So when the orders came to induct one MI8 aircraft into Sri Lanka with the IPKF, he became the chosen one and landed at Palaly on 15 September 1987.

As he walked down the stairs from his room, he saw the LTTE members coming in. He had flown some of the EPRLF fighters from Palaly to Trinco several times, but never the LTTE guys. He had not seen any of them until now and was surprised to realise that they looked like any of the Sri Lankan Tamils. The larger-than-life image that they had built about themselves was a myth, he thought.

He stepped out of the building with his rucksack and saw Major Sheonan Singh of the 10 Para Commando battalion standing outside with his men, armed with carbines and the SLRs. They were all dressed up in the recently introduced disruptive pattern uniform. Prakash had conducted many night drop exercises with the Para Commandoes who were also stationed in Jodhpur and knew Sheonan well.

Prakash walked past him, throwing a glance at him and smiling. Sheonan just looked through him.

There were about twenty soldiers with Sheonan and all of them were armed. On the other side of the building, he saw the Sri Lankan armed soldiers standing on guard. His soldierly instinct told him that something was not right here. He walked on towards his new home.

As the 1-ton with the LTTE operatives entered the airport premises, a brigadier of the Sri Lankan Army started shouting orders to the captain.

'Get these sons of ******* down', he shouted.

'Yes, Sir', the captain replied.

Pulendran and Kumar lead the group, and they did not look bothered in the least. The swagger in their walk said it all. They looked at the Indian soldiers and smiled at them knowingly, appearing reassured among them.

Prakash walked into the building that was to be his home for the rest of his stay in Palaly and switched on the television to find out if the capture of the LTTE fighters was making big news. It was. The only television station, the Sri Lanka Broadcasting service, was flashing the news that eighteen LTTE fighters, along with their commanders Pulendran and Kumar, had been arrested by the Sri Lankan Navy, along with a large haul of arms and ammunition, while returning from India.

The President, Mr Jayewardene, later in his address to the nation, declared that the transportation of the arms and ammunition was in serious contravention to the peace accord, and the LTTE fighters would be tried by a military court in Colombo. To support his claim, he also promised to get them to Colombo, to present them before the international media. The international media persons wanted everything to take place in Colombo. They never dared to move out of the comfortable confines of their luxury hotels, due to fear of reprisal. Nearly all reporting on Sri Lanka was happening from their hotel rooms.

At the Jaffna University military headquarters of the LTTE, Parabhakaran was furious when he saw the President's broadcast. Seated on either side were Kittu, his second-in-command, and Mahattaya, his political wing commander who was also the stand-in second-in-command, in Kittu's absence. He looked at them and said, 'Under no circumstances should they be handed over to the Sri Lankan Army. They will torture them and coerce them to state whatever they want to in front of the international media. We will be exposed and international opinions will go against us. From being the oppressed we will become known as the perpetrators of violence in Sri Lanka'.

Kittu and Mahattaya nodded in agreement.

'What should we do?', asked Kittu.

'We cannot plan and execute a rescue operation, because the Palaly airport is heavily fortified and guarded by the SLAF', replied Mahattaya, the more experienced fighter of the two.

'Maybe we can bribe the SLAF commander at Palaly and get our fighters out', Kittu suggested.

'Ha, you think that is a possibility? With the amount of poison they have against us, it is no use even attempting it.'

'Get me Dixit, I will speak to him', said Prabhakaran after a thought.

The LTTE had the latest, most sophisticated communication equipment and network available at that time. With VHF radio sets being patched onto telephone lines and ranges up to 300 km, through coded communication, they could speak nearly anywhere they desired in the world. Influential Sri Lankan and Indian-origin Tamils all over the world supported the LTTE, both morally and financially. They had, over a period of time, procured and sent the latest and best of the international market to them. Communication hubs, by way of HAM sets and the VHF transmission stations, had been set up clandestinely in the houses and offices of these supporters, in India and other countries in the west. The LTTE had a very covert and sophisticated system for the procurement of arms, communication equipment, and ammunition.

Mahattaya got up, picked up the VHF radio set that was lying on the table across the room, and brought it to

Prabhakaran. He stepped out of the room and went into the adjoining room that was their communication centre and told the operator there to put a call through to the Indian High Commissioner in Colombo.

Jyotindra Nath Dixit loved his evening brandy as much as he loved his cigar. Born in Madras to a Malayali couple, he got his surname 'Dixit' from his stepfather. A well-read individual with years of international diplomatic experience behind him, he was Rajiv Gandhi's man and had been handpicked by him as Indian High Commissioner to Sri Lanka. He had been instrumental in forging strong ties with Bangladesh just after the country's creation and was a shrewd diplomat who Rajiv Gandhi thought could handle Jayewardene well.

Prabhakaran and Dixit shared a warm relationship that went back as far as 1980 when they had first met in Madras.

'You are aware that eighteen of my men have been captured by the SLAF', Prabhakaran started, matter-of-factly.

'Yes', Dixit replied in a flat voice that promised nothing.

'I want them out Dixit', said Prabhakaran.

'Let me talk to Jayewardene and get back to you.'

'Do whatever has to be done but they should not be handed over to the SLAF or the Sri Lankan government. I hope you understand that it is not only dangerous for me, but you too. The SLAF will torture them and make them state in front of the international media how India is supporting us covertly in our fight for the Tamil Eelam, which may not be liked by Mr Rajiv Gandhi. I hope you understand', Prabhakaran said, dropping a veiled threat.

Son of a b****, thought Dixit.

'Yes, I understand. Let me speak to the PM'. The bastard is actually threatening me, Dixit thought as he put down the receiver.

He relit his cigar, took in a deep puff, blew out the smoke, and picked up the receiver again.

'Get me the Special Secretary to the President of Sri Lanka', he told the operator of the High Commission.

'Yes, Sir', replied the operator in her chirpy voice.

'Mr President, good evening. I heard your address to the nation, and I must compliment you for the swiftness of action by the SLAF and for your bold announcement to get them to justice', Dixit said in flattery.

'I have learnt all this from you Mr Dixit', Jayewardene replied diplomatically, but Dixit could smell the hint of sarcasm in it. They were correct in calling him the 'Old fox', Dixit concluded.

'I have a request to make, which I hope you will accept in the larger interest of the friendship between India and Sri Lanka.'

'Let me hear it. I cannot promise you anything now', said Jayewardene, anticipating what was coming.

'Please do not bring the LTTE boys to Colombo to be presented in front of the media. It will further deteriorate the fragile peace and surrender of arms, as per the peace accord', replied Dixit.

'I have already announced it on national television Mr Dixit, and I cannot go back on my word', he said.

'Mr President', started Dixit again, 'please listen to me, we have to find a way out', he pleaded.

'There is a way out Mr Dixit, as is in all problems that we face. You can take the prisoners into your custody and announce that India will try them as per international norms, for going against the accord. Punish them. Show the world that you are with the GoSL. Once you agree to do this, I will announce it on national television. This way, I will have kept my word and will not have to be embarrassed in front of the media, and you will demonstrate to the world that you are not with the terrorists, but with the democratically elected, legitimate government of Sri Lanka. How does that sound to you?', Jayewardene replied.

Now, this put Dixit in a quandary.

Shrewd man, Dixit thought. Jayewardene had already considered this and wanted India to get involved in arresting and prosecuting the LTTE fighters in the Indian courts.

This would drive a wedge of suspicion between them and would ensure that the heat shifted onto the IPKF.

He knew full well that there was no other way to get them out of this mess.

'Thank you, Sir, I will convey your advice to the Honourable Prime Minister of India and await his decision', he replied.

'He will listen to what you say and you know that. Nevertheless, follow the protocol', Jaywardene chuckled.

'Yes, Sir', replied Dixit, and the secured line went dead.

'Get me the Prime Minister. Tell his secretary that it is important, and no matter where he is, I need to talk to him', He told his first secretary in the High Commission.

'Okay Dixit ji, I understand the gist of what you are saying. I am meeting the CMC tomorrow and I will let you know about any further action that needs to be taken', the PM casually replied, when Dixit spoke to him on the secure line.

The PM definitely did not understand the criticality of the situation, and despite the High Commissioner's detailed analysis of what could happen in the future, he had postponed the decision-making by another twenty-four hours. That is how the PMO functions nowadays. Postpone, postpone, and forget.

'But Mr Prime Minister I would request…'

'Dixit ji, handle it until then, best of luck'. *Click.* The line went dead.

Dixit had no option but to wait and hope that the LTTE, the SLAF, or even the IPKF, did not do anything stupid.

DIXIT'S DILEMMA

CHAPTER 2

DON'T KNOW HOW TO HANDLE THE SITUATION

Pulendran and Kumar entered the lounge, with the other sixteen LTTE men following them.

'This is where you all will stay until further orders', the SLAF Captain said and then went away.

Sheonan and his team moved in closer to the building, forming the inner cordon.

The SLAF team quickly formed an outer cordon around them and moved in four OT-64 SKOTs to take up position all around the building. The SKOT were amphibious, armoured personnel carriers that had recently been acquired by the SLAF from Czechoslovakia as the LTTE ambushes and snipers had become extremely potent and accurate, and the SLAF had suffered many casualties.

Sheonan observed that the SLAF personnel were

better equipped than the Indian Para Commandoes, who were the so-called 'Elite' of the Indian Army but were still carrying the vintage 9mm CMG and the 7.62mm SLR. The former was an improved version of the original Sterling submachine gun of the 1953 range, and the latter a WWII-era rifle. The SLAF had AKs and Uzis.

Orders were still not clear regarding whether the LTTE men would be handed over to the SLAF or kept under guard by the IPKF. The SLAF was getting restless and wanted the men in their custody.

Sometime during the next day, the eighteen LTTE operatives were moved into the heptr hangers across the service track.

The President of Sri Lanka appeared again on the national state-controlled television channel, Rupavahini, and announced that the LTTE men would be brought to Colombo and presented before the media. Dixit, who was watching the news, jumped up from his office chair and picked up the phone to get through to the President.

'Sorry Mr Dixit, His Excellency is in a meeting, and just between you and me, he will not be interested in speaking to you', informed his Special Secretary, who had stepped out of the meeting to speak to him.

'You must insist that I wish to speak to him', pleaded Dixit.

'Sorry Sir, I may not be able to help you. Good day', the Special Secretary replied.

'But…well, thank you', Dixit conceded.

He knew it was no use trying to press any further. He decided to go personally to meet the President.

As he stepped inside the Presidential palace office of Jayewardene, he could sense that he was not a welcome guest. The Special Secretary was visibly upset to see him and asked him, rather rudely, about the purpose of his visit.

'Well, I am thankful to you and greatly appreciate the effort that you have made to convince the President to talk to me over the phone, but unfortunately, due to his very busy schedule, he could not. So I thought I would come here myself, and explain the disastrous consequences of bringing the LTTE men to Colombo and presenting them in front of the press', was Dixit's sugar-coated reply.

Dixit was one of the best Indian diplomats of his era and he had dealt with many such arrogant 'more-loyal-than-the-king' loyalists, in India and abroad.

The Special Secretary opened his mouth to speak but shut it immediately as he saw the President walking down the long corridor from his residential quarters.

Junius Richard Jayewardene, commonly abbreviated in Sri Lanka as J.R. With more than fifty years of political experience, and at eighty years of age, J.R. was a savvy politician par excellence, and at least in the sub-continent at that point of time, he was the best. He would remain unperturbed in the worst of times, and calm and composed during the best. A man who displayed very few emotions, he was sophisticated and well-educated, which was due to his upbringing in a prominent well-to-do family. He was the twelfth child of his parents. His father was a prominent and influential lawyer and his mother was the daughter of a wealthy merchant. He had been the leader of the nationalist movement in Ceylon, as it was then known, and had served in a variety of cabinet positions in the decades following independence.

A long-time member of the United National Party, he had led it to a landslide victory in 1977 and served as Prime Minister for half a year before becoming the country's first executive president under an amended constitution.

Dixit was aware that Jayewardene was a controversial figure in the history of Sri Lanka, his actions have been recognized as having significantly contributed to the beginnings of the Sri Lankan Civil War. Following the 1983 anti-Tamil riots in Sri Lanka, carried out by Sinhalese mobs that caused between 400 to 3,000 Tamil deaths, Jayewardene distanced himself from the riots and did not attempt to stop the continuous attacks on the Tamils. Criticized for his handling of the tensions between the

Tamils and Sinhalese, Jayewardene had notoriously said in the Daily Telegraph, 'Really, if I starve the Tamils out, the Sinhala people will be happy'.

Jayewardene was immaculately dressed in his white *sarama* (Dhoti or sarong-like clothing), a full-sleeved white shirt, and black leather sandals. His strides always portrayed a man with a purpose. He was tall and well-built, with intelligent eyes and a prominent nose. His hair was neatly combed back, and his complete demeanour demonstrated a man of immense confidence and emotional control.

The Presidential palace, or the President's house as it is known, has been the official residence and workplace of the President of Sri Lanka since 1972, prior to which it was known as the King's or Queen's house. It is divided into two wings, the offices and the residential wing, joined by a long open corridor that travels through 'Gordon's Garden', named after one of the pre-independence governor-generals of Sri Lanka. A remnant of colonial-era architecture, the palace had, over the years, gone through many renovations and reconstructions. On assuming office, Jayewardene refurbished the palace under the supervision of renowned architect Geoffery Bawa, who was born to a Muslim father and Catholic mother.

'Good morning Mr Dixit, nice to see you', he greeted loudly from the corridor. Raised by an English nanny, J.R.

spoke English fluently with a British accent.

'Good morning, Your Excellency', Dixit replied, bending forward from his waist upwards.

'What brings you here so early in the morning? Have you come to meet me?', asked Jayewardene rather curiously, not breaking his stride as he walked past Dixit.

'Yes, Your Excellency', Dixit replied, quickly following and matching his steps.

'Come along. Let's have a nice cup of Sri Lankan tea together', he replied and walked into his office.

Dixit looked at the Special Secretary and smiled. He looked away.

The President waited for the steward to pour the tea and leave.

'Mr Dixit, I think I know why you are here. And pre-empting you, I will say that I have decided what I have decided, and that will not change. Don't worry, now that you are here, I will still hear you out – and off the records, it will only be between you and me', he said.

'Your Excellency, your announcement about getting the captured LTTE men to Colombo has not gone down well with Prabhakaran and we will have serious repercussions in implementing the peace accord', he started.

'You think that at this time I should be worried about what Prabhakaran thinks or says? Are you trying to frighten me?', the President asked, rather politely.

'Not for one moment Sir', Dixit replied earnestly and continued, 'You are aware, Your Excellency, that the peace accord is, at the moment, in a very fragile state. We do not want the accord to fail. If you get the LTTE men to Colombo and present them in front of the international media, it will surely upset Prabhakaran, and then the accord is bound to fail. We do not want this to happen, do we?', Dixit said, leaving the statement open-ended.

'So what do you want me to do? Let these LTTE men get off scot-free and allow them to keep inducting arms and ammunition supplied by your government into Jaffna, to fight and kill my men? I am sorry, this will not happen, especially now that I have announced their presentation in front of international media on national television. I cannot go back on my word', Jayewardene replied, a wee bit of anger creeping into his voice.

'But Your Excellency, you are aware that the onus of implementation of this peace accord lies with the Indian government, and therefore, on behalf of the Government of India, I am making a formal request to handover the LTTE men to the IPKF so that as a gesture of solidarity with the LTTE, we can further negotiate with them. We are presently in a very precarious situation and would not like this to escalate further', pleaded Dixit.

'Mr Dixit, I do not think that I can help you any further in this matter. What is said is said, and I will not go back on my word. You may convey this, with all humility and respect, to His Excellency, Mr Rajiv Gandhi, the Prime Minister of India', Jayewardene concluded, getting up from his seat, indicating the end of the conversation.

Dixit had no option but to get up, bow his head to gesture goodbye, and walk out of the room.

He had gambled for a commitment from the President without the official clearance from Rajiv Gandhi. Now his only option was to convince the PM to take over the LTTE prisoners by force from the SLAF if need be.

Dixit rushed back to the Indian High Commission located at Galle road, about 5 kilometres from the Presidential palace. 'Get me Mr Raja, Special Secretary to the Prime Minister immediately', he told his secretary as he stepped inside the building.

'Sorry Sir, he is in a meeting and will be available only after two o'clock', she informed him on the intercom a few minutes later.

'Okay, keep the call pending and whenever he, or the Prime Minister, is available put the call through.'

What is the PM planning to do? If something happens to the LTTE men or if there is an armed confrontation between the IPKF and SLAF, we are going to be in a lot of trouble. The PM has to make a decision before it is too late, Dixit thought.

Known to only a handful of Rajiv Gandhi loyalists and the coterie, he had not even consulted his cabinet before deciding to induct the IPKF into the island country. Then, with over-ambitious civil and military officers eager to please him, the IPKF was sent in without preparations. History was in the making.

It was around 1000 hours on 5 October, when Captain Ranjit Singh Bhadauriya, returning from Trincomalee, stepped out of the An-32 with his team.

His veteran JCO standing next to him said, 'Sir, do you see what I am seeing?'

'Yes I do', replied Ranjit.

'Something is not right here Sir. Major Sheonan's team appears posted around the airport ATC building and around them are the SLAF. What is going on?', Subedar Mellu Ram asked.

'Yes, it does seem very odd to me too. Don't worry, with Major Sheonan in command there I am sure all is okay', said Ranjit. He walked straight towards the tents where the teams were staying.

On seeing Ranjit walking towards the tents, Sheonan also joined him.

'So how was your stay at Trinco?', he asked.

'Fine Sir, some riots had broken out due to the Indo-Sri Lanka accord, and they wanted some additional troops', replied Ranjit.

'But you tell me Sir, what's happening here? Seems like a lot of action. You in the inner cordon and the SLAF around you', Ranjit continued, seeming oblivious to the recent developments.

'You better get your team ready to take over the duties from my team. We have been here for the last twenty-four hours and need to be relieved', Sheonan said.

'Wilco Sir, but what's happening here? At least give me a run-down.'

'You remember the day you left, 2 October. The SLAF arrested eighteen LTTE men the next day', Sheonan said.

'Yes Sir, I know that, and the arrested LTTE fighters include Pulendran and Kumar. That's why the riots in Trinco escalated further', Ranjit replied.

'Now, even after forty-two hours, we still have not received clear orders on whether they will remain with us or be handed over to the SLAF. The situation is getting tenser by the minute. Jayewardene has already declared that these LTTE men will be transported to Colombo and presented in front of the international press. Prabhakaran does not want this to happen. Until clear orders are received, we will remain in this mode.'

'Great Sir, Give me ten minutes, I will get my team together, brief them, and start taking over from you', he replied.

As Ranjit moved towards his team's tents, he could now hear some SA firing and mortar shells exploding, in and around the airfield. He looked enquiringly towards Sheonan.

'Yes, the LTTE has started firing at the SLAF and our positions. Be careful', Sheonan cautioned, understanding Ranjit's predicament.

'Sir', said a soldier standing outside their tent.

'Yes, what is it Sohan?', Sheonan asked.

'Sir, the Col GS 54 Div wants to speak to you immediately.'

'Okay, I will take the call here. Put it through.'

'Good afternoon, Sir', Sheonan said, answering the call.

Gesturing to Ranjit to come back and stand closer, 'Stay on the listening watch', he whispered to Ranjit, covering the mouthpiece.

'Good afternoon, Sheonan', Colonel Hoshiyar Singh replied. 'Listen carefully, no decision has been made on the LTTE men and we fear that the SLAF may try to forcibly take them to Colombo. They have an aircraft ready on the runway. I want you to block the runway immediately to make sure that the aircraft cannot take off until we get further orders and I tell you to clear the runway. You will not take orders from anyone else. Is that understood?'

'To also give you an update on what is happening around us', he continued, 'On the fourth, there was a large-scale slaughter of Sinhalese civilians by the LTTE, and a few SLAF soldiers have been held hostage by them.'

'Wilco Sir. The runway has to be blocked so that the aircraft does not take off', Sheonan repeated the orders, making sure that Ranjit on the listening watch knew what the call was all about.

'Yes, and do it fast. Once it is done, confirm it to me', replied Hoshiyar.

'Wilco sir', Sheonan said and put the receiver down.

'You see Ranjit, how fluid the situation is here. No one really knows what is going to happen. Let's place a 1-ton truck in front and a Jonga at the rear end of the aircraft', he said, picking up his weapon.

Sheonan and Ranjit rushed out and jumped inside the Jonga parked outside their tent.

'Mellu Ram sahib, get the 1-ton and four buddy pairs and follow us', shouted Ranjit to Mellu Ram, who was getting the team together.

'Yes Sir', Mellu Ram replied. He quickly ordered four of the buddy pairs standing close by to get in the 1-ton which was parked nearby and drove off behind the Jonga.

The 1-ton truck had just arrived a few days ago from Jodhpur. The Paratroopers had moved in with a Nissan Jonga and a Royal Enfield motorcycle when they were inducted in July.

Both the vehicles sped towards the aircraft parked at the end of the runway.

They drove the Jonga right under the cockpit of the aircraft and parked it in front of the nose wheel. The 1-ton was then parked behind the aircraft at an angle, ensuring that the aircraft could not reverse and take off. Ranjit then assigned four commandoes to stand guard along with the vehicles.

'Hey, hey, hey what do you guys think you are doing?', the perturbed pilot, who was doing his pre-take-off checks, asked.

'Blocking your take off', Sheonan said, matter-of-factly.

'You can't do that', the pilot protested.

'Yes we can and we have', Sheonan declared.

'I will have to inform the ATC.'

'Go ahead, inform them, just in case they have not seen it yet.' Sheonan turned towards the ATC, which was about 50 metres from where this conversation was taking place.

The pilot got into the aircraft, put his headset on, and reported his situation to the ATC.

'Red Arrow to Palaly.'

'Red Arrow, go ahead', the ATC replied.

'Red Arrow the runway has been blocked by the IPKF. Repeat, runway blocked by IPKF.'

The ATC had no answer. The officer there just repeated the pilot's reporting.

'Red Arrow runway blocked by IPKF, yes I can see it', the ATC officer said.

'Red Arrow what am I supposed to do?', the pilot asked.

'Red Arrow, don't know', the ATC officer replied.

'Red Arrow, move your butt and find out', the pilot was agitated now.

'Red Arrow, no one presently available at ATC. I will call Base Ops and check.'

The pilot looked out of the cockpit window and could not see any of the commandoes. He thought they may have left after they saw him making the call to the ATC. He took off his headset and turned around to leave the cockpit.

Two of the commandoes stood right behind him, inside the cockpit.

'Remain seated, Captain', Ranjit said.

The pilot was so surprised that he just slumped in his seat.

'Mellu Ram Sahab, keep him here', Ranjit told Subedar Mellu Ram.

'Yes Sir', Mellu smiled at Ranjit.

'Let's go to the hanger where the LTTE men have been shifted to. You can take over the duties and relieve my team', Sheonan said.

They crossed the runway, but before entering the hanger that stood close to the ATC, they waved at the same officer inside. Not knowing what to do, he just waved back.

Ranjit counted all eighteen LTTE men, nodded to Sheonan, and told his company havildar major (CHM) to start taking over the positions held by the previous team.

The light machine gun (LMG) was deployed at the window, and Ranjit put an additional 84MM Carl Gustav rocket launcher in a make-shift emplacement made out of sandbags, next to the building.

'Be careful', Sheonan said, 'I hope I can take a bath before the next assignment comes in, see you', he smiled and left.

'See you Sir', Ranjit saluted.

Sheonan walked up to the telephone outside the hanger and called Colonel Hoshiyar.

'Task completed Sir', he reported.

'Good.'

Sheonan and his team slowly walked back to their tents.

The Palaly airfield was spread over approximately 10 sq kms. It was bound by four roads in all the cardinal directions; Jaffna-Poonalai-Point Pedro to its north, Vallai

Tellipalai Araly road to the south, a lateral joining both these roads towards the east, and road Kadduv Myllidy in the west. Between the lateral and the airfield was a pro-LTTE settlement. The airfield was surrounded by a 12 feet high barbed wire fencing with twelve 15 feet guard posts that were manned with LMGs around the clock. To the southwest and northwest side was a dense jungle that was a source of constant worry for the SLAF. The runway was aligned southwest to northeast. To the north lay the Palk Strait in the Indian Ocean.

Palaly, in itself, was a non-descriptive village with a population of about 200 people, spread over a large area with agriculture as their main occupation. But they were strong supporters of the LTTE ideology and would act as overground workers or sympathisers whenever required.

With the situation fast deteriorating, the SLAF had deployed their SKOTs around the airfield to ward off any attempt by the LTTE to rush the airfield and take over the ATC. The road from the main gate, which was to the east, came up to the ATC. To the north of the airfield, the field hospital of the SLAF stood, and next to it, the Div HQ. The Para Commandoes tents were pitched on the end of the runway, not too far from the MI8 helicopter base. They often had to hold on to their tents whenever the heptrs either took off or landed.

The airfield was of strategic importance for sustaining operations in the Jaffna peninsula, and as such, was heavily fortified and guarded.

Dixit was now on the verge of a panic attack. Two days had gone by and no decision had been shared by the PM. He had spoken to him today, but the PM had postponed it to the next day again. Precious days were being lost and the situation was fast becoming explosive.

Suddenly, his phone rang.

His secretary was on the line.

'It's Prabhakaran', she informed him.

'What have you told him?', asked Dixit, in an attempt to avoid speaking to him.

'He has eyes and ears on us, Sir, he told me not to even try to make that excuse. He knows that you entered the office at 10:20 am', she replied.

'Bloody hell, so much for being the High Commissioner of India. Put him through.'

'Mr Dixit, you are making a fool of me and I do not like it', started Prabhakaran.

'No no, how can you even think of that. We are good friends. I am trying to help you but the GoSL is not cooperating. You know how adamant Jayewardene can be. He is just not budging from his stand', Dixit replied diplomatically.

'I think we need to meet today.'

'Sure, why not?', Dixit confirmed, hoping to buy time until a decision came from Delhi.

'Okay, today three o'clock, at 54 Div HQ Palaly', Prabhakaran said.

'I will see you there.'

Dixit landed at Palaly airport exactly at 2:30 pm and found the GOC Major General Harkirat 'Harry' Singh waiting on the tarmac.

'It is a dangerous situation and we have to deal with Prabhakaran very patiently and diplomatically', Dixit said as they walked to the waiting Jonga.

'I understand Sir', replied Harry.

Dixit and Harry were not on cordial personal or professional terms. Harry was of the opinion that Dixit was playing into the hands of the LTTE, and Dixit thought Harry was not a ground soldier.

'Do not commit to anything until we get orders from Delhi. The PM has still not made up his mind, and I can understand his predicament. He is stuck between the devil and the deep sea. Let's try to negotiate some more time for him to decide.'

Dixit was a Gandhi loyalist and had been in their good books since the time of Mrs Indira Gandhi, which is why he had been hand-picked by Rajeev Gandhi as the Indian High Commissioner to Sri Lanka.

They drove in silence to the make-shift officers' mess of the Div HQs, enclosed in a small building adjoining the offices of the Division.

Col Hoshiyar Singh was waiting to receive them as they stepped out of the Jonga.

'He is already here', said Hoshiyar, referring to the arrival of Prabhakaran

'Good', Dixit replied.

Prabhakaran did not get up on seeing Dixit when the latter entered the mess.

'Hello Mr Prabhakaran, nice to see you here', Dixit greeted.

Prabhakaran did not acknowledge his salutation. He was visibly upset and seemed like a man who was trying to suppress his anger.

'I know and understand that you are upset about the developments of the last few days', continued Dixit, 'and we are here to solve the problem. I am sure that in the next two or three days, we will be able to resolve the issue.'

'Two-three days will be too late Mr Dixit', Prabhakaran retorted, 'we need to resolve it now before I leave', Prabhakaran looked at Hoshiyar.

'Mr Prabhakaran is of the view that the LTTE operatives

presently at Palaly airport must be released or handed over to the IPKF, and all further actions should be taken by the Government of India and not by the GoSL', said Hoshiyar, who had already spoken to Prabhakaran earlier.

'This decision can only be taken by the Honourable Prime Minister of India. I will convey your message to him. I am confident that we will receive a reply in two or three days, as he will have to consider the views of all the stakeholders', Dixit replied.

'We do not have much time. The GoSL will move the fighters from here to Colombo. This should not happen under any circumstances. If this happens, it will be very bad for the accord, and for the both of us', warned Prabhakaran.

'We are trying our best under the provisions of the peace accord Mr Prabhakaran, whatever can be done will be done.'

'I do not care what the accord says. It is between you and the GoSL. I only want my tigers to be released or handed over to the IPKF. Under no circumstances will they be handed over to the GoSL. In case that happens, I will be a very upset man and that will not be good for any of us', Prabhakaran said, and before the conversation could go any further, he got up and walked out of the mess, got into the Jonga that had brought him, and left.

Dixit and Harkirat knew that Prabhakaran's threat was

not an empty one.

'I think we don't have much of a choice', Dixit stated.

'I agree with you', Harkirat replied.

'So what's your problem, take over the LTTE operatives from the SLAF', Dixit suggested.

'Sorry Sir, I get my orders from the army headquarters.'

'I, by virtue of being the Indian High Commissioner in Sri Lanka, give you executive orders to take over the LTTE operatives and place them in your custody. These orders may be construed to be given on behalf of the Honourable Prime Minister of India', said a visibly upset Dixit.

'I am sorry I will not take orders from you. My orders come from, and on behalf of, the COAS through HQ Southern Command and the Adhoc HQ at Madras, and that is how it shall be.'

Harry came from one of the well-known battalions of an elite regiment of the Indian Army, and he knew his protocols well. He could not be bullied into accepting orders, not even from the High Commissioner of India; not until he was placed under his command, or until he had specific orders to do so. Presently, he had neither.

'This may not go down well with the PMO', Dixit warned, actually meaning the PM.

'May not. But protocol is protocol', an adamant Harry replied.

'Okay then, I will come back to you with specific orders, or you will get the same orders from your channel. Listening to me would have saved us some precious hours.'

'We have a sumptuous lunch laid out for you, kindly join us', Harry said, cutting short the conversation.

'Thank you, but I do not have lunch. I will fly back to Colombo now', he replied.

'Hoshiyar, please call for the High Commissioner's Jonga, and see him off at the tarmac', Harry told the Col GS.

'My pleasure Sir', he replied.

'Hoshiyar, I will be waiting for you at the lunch table', Harry added.

Dixit was a troubled man. The situation in Sri Lanka was getting explosive with every passing minute, and if the LTTE men were taken to Colombo, or the LTTE decided to attack and free their men, it would be catastrophic. And there was still no decision being taken by the Indian government.

The Col GS saluted goodbye to him, which Dixit did not acknowledge, as he was still deep in his thoughts as he boarded the aircraft to Colombo.

Why were Indian military vehicles parked in front of a Sri Lankan aircraft, he thought, as his aircraft left the runway.

Unknown to Dixit, the PM had not even consulted

his cabinet prior to agreeing to the Indo-Sri Lanka peace accord. Everyone thought Rajiv Gandhi was a novice, and in the years to come, he did not prove them wrong.

Rajiv Gandhi was only forty years old when he became the PM of India. His mother, Indira Gandhi, and grandfather, J.L. Nehru, were forty-eight and fifty-seven years old respectively when they took over as the PM of India. He was a typical dynast, struggling to measure up to a legacy and leave a permanent stamp.

Starting his schooling from Welham preparatory, moving to Doon School, and then on to the Imperial College, London, he had always revelled in science and engineering rather than political science or philosophy. He dreamt practically.

Of medium build with a receding hairline now, he was soft-spoken and preferred consensus to individual decision-making. By profession, he was an airline pilot and would have wanted to stay as such, but the sudden demise of his younger politician brother, Sanjay Gandhi, abruptly ended his flying career and forced him into the murky waters of Indian politics.

Reluctantly, in the initial years, he had no choice but to accept the mantle of PM after a thumping election victory, riding on the sympathy wave of his mother's assassination.

Since then, his tenure as the PM had been a roller

coaster ride. One with a few ups and many downs. He had hoped that the Indo-Sri Lanka Peace Accord would add a feather to his cap. It had been many years since India clandestinely trained various separatist groups in Sri Lanka. It was his mother's initiative to intervene in Sri Lanka, with an aim to please the Tamilians; more of a political decision rather than an emotional one. In the case of Sri Lanka, what swayed his judgement, and his mother's, was not their ethnic affections, but the compulsion of Tamil Nadu politics, which would eventually prove to be his waterloo.

He was aware that the cadres of LTTE, PLOTE, EPRLF, and a few others were being trained by the R&AW. The director of R&AW, J.N Verma, had briefed him on the training camps spread from Chakrata in the Garhwal Himalayas, to the dense coconut and rubber plantations in Tamil Nadu.

The influx of thousands of refugees from the northern province of Jaffna in Sri Lanka had created a Bangladesh-like scenario in India and forced Rajiv Gandhi to act sternly but diplomatically to handle the situation. Jayewardene was initially reluctant to agree to a peace accord but Operation Poonamalai forced him to change his stance.

Rajiv Gandhi was satisfied with the doings and happenings in Sri Lanka but was this the calm before the storm, he wondered.

'Call Mr A.K. Verma over immediately', he told his

Special PA, dispelling negative thoughts. Verma had been the R&AW director since Rajiv Gandhi had taken over as the PM. He was known to be a hard taskmaster, which the PM desired to be, but was not. Verma did not bother to be politically correct or popular, he left that to the politicians. He had to get the work done, mostly dirty work. His tremendous insight into the political situation, particularly in the Indian sub-continent, was impressive by all standards.

'Verma ji, give me a brief on the LTTE operatives that have been arrested by the SLAF and also advise me on the actions that we should take. Dixit ji is in a dilemma and awaiting my directions on whether we should take them in our custody or hand them over to the Sri Lankans', he told Verma, the moment he entered his office.

'Well Sir, the LTTE operatives were ferrying arms and ammunition from Rameshwaram to Point Pedro in Sri Lanka when they were intercepted and arrested by the Sri Lankan Navy. They are now under the guard of the IPKF, at the Palaly airfield in Jaffna. Mr Jayewardene wants them in Colombo, where he intends to present them in front of the international media, to prove that they have violated the peace accord and that India is providing military assistance to them. When Dixit ji met him, he suggested that we take over and hold a trial as per international laws to try separatists, which for obvious reasons we cannot do', said Verma, in brief.

'That is the problem, what is the solution?', the PM asked.

'I have spoken to Prabhakaran and, fortunately, he understands our predicament. He has suggested that in the eventuality of our having to hand the LTTE operatives to SLAF, he will manage the situation, although he is very upset with us', said Verma.

'Do you think this could lead to a backlash? Such as an armed confrontation with the LTTE?', asked the PM.

'Sir, they are our boys, they will not fight against us.'

CYANIDE CAPSULE: DEATH IN SAPADH

CHAPTER 3

PRABHAKARAN VOWS REVENGE

Ranjit had finished his round of the defensive positions taken up by his team and passed on instructions to stay alert and make sure the SLAF personnel did not get anywhere near the building that housed the LTTE fighters.

It was nearing lunch time and as was routine, the lunch, known as *sapadh* in Tamil, for the LTTE operatives arrived by human courier from the adjoining village.

The couriers walked up to Ranjit, and through their interpreter who was accompanying them, told him that they had brought lunch for the 'Tigers'.

Two pre-puberty boys, who were the human couriers, had nineteen rolled-up banana leaves, eighteen of which had rice and sambar, while the nineteenth one had cyanide capsules, a string tied to each one of them. Ranjit recognised the cyanide capsules that the LTTE fighters wore around their necks, ones they would chew when capture or torture was imminent.

Each of the cyanide capsules was the size of a 7.62×51mm cartridge. The cartridge-like capsule had two compartments; one had the potassium cyanide powder, and the other acid. As the LTTE operatives bit into the capsule, the acid would burn the inner cheek skin and the powder would immediately be absorbed into the bloodstream, thereby killing the LTTE operative within seconds.

Ranjit looked up at the interpreter, and pointing towards the capsules, asked, 'Why this?'

The interpreter asked the two boys in Tamil.

'They say they have been instructed to do so by their commander', the interpreter translated the reply given by the two boys.

'And who is their commander?', Ranjit asked.

'They do not know, the message came to them by another courier.'

'Wait', he told them.

He walked to the nearby phone and called up the Colonel General Staff.

'Sir, the *sapadh* that has come for the LTTE guys has eighteen cyanide capsules with it. The couriers insist that it must go in. What are the orders for me?', asked Ranjit.

'Ranjit, just hold the line', said the Col GS. Ranjit could hear a distorted conversation on the other side.

'It's Capt Ranjit of the Paras Sir', said the Col GS, addressing the GOC sitting across his desk, 'the *sapadh* for the LTTE guys also has cyanide capsules. Should we let it go in?', he asked.

'Tell Ranjit that you will call him in a while, until then, he should not let the *sapadh* go in', replied the GOC.

'Ranjit, I will call you in a while. Don't let the *sapadh* go in, hold those guys also', the Col GS said as he passed on the GOC's instructions.

'Hoshiyar, it is a tricky situation', the GOC started, as he put the handset down. 'Prabhakaran knows that sometime during the day, the Government of India will hand over the LTTE fighters to the SLAF. He has, in anticipation, instructed his commander here to send the cyanide capsules with the food, so that they do not remain alive to give the media a statement. As far as Mr Dixit is concerned, he is not going to get any instructions from the PMO, and neither are we. So, someone has to make a decision. If we let them go, they will be made to sing like a canary by the SLAF, and Prabhakaran will be very upset with us'.

'That's true Sir', said Hoshiyar.

'We cannot hold them any longer as the SLAF is getting restive and aggressive, and I do not want to have a showdown with them', continued the GOC. 'Get me Prabhakaran.'

'General, let the cyanide capsules go in. You do not know that there are cyanide capsules with the *sapadh*', Prabhakaran said.

'I understand', replied Harkirat.

He looked up at Hoshiyar, 'You heard what Prabhakaran said, inform Ranjit accordingly', then the GOC and walked out of the Col GS's office.

Ranjit was surprised by the decision to let the capsules go in, but orders were orders and he, as a junior officer, needed to obey them.

All the nineteen rolled banana leaves were allowed to go in with the couriers, who kept them at the door and left the area in a hurry.

Ranjit was looking at the LTTE operatives. A few of them got up and began distributing the *sapadh* leaves, along with a cyanide capsule, to each one of them. Once done, they all wore the cyanide capsules around their necks and sat down to form a square and have their food.

Pulendran and Kumar had taken two capsules each, maybe to ensure their deaths. Being senior commanders, they did not want to be taken alive by the SLAF. The two remaining LTTE operatives were told to share capsules with two others.

It was around 4 o'clock when Ranjit got a call from the Col GS.

'Ranjit, withdraw your team and return to your tents. I repeat, withdraw your team and return to your tents. Is that understood?'

'I will withdraw my team from where the LTTE operatives are kept, and we will return to our tents. Roger Sir', repeated Ranjit.

'You are correct. You may log my orders', the Col GS replied.

'Wilco Sir'

He would log it later after reaching the tents.

Ranjit moved outside the hanger, blew a whistle, and raised his right hand over his head, moving it in a clockwise direction four times, and then pointing in front of him. It was a signal for the team to collect in front of him.

Within seconds, the team lifted all their weapons and equipment and stood in threes in front of him.

'Move back to your tents, NOW', he said and started walking in the direction of the tents.

The SLAF, on seeing this, immediately moved into the hanger and took over the positions vacated by the Paras.

Prakash entered the hanger just when this melee was

taking place; no one really had their eyes on him. It was by chance, not by deliberate action, he had no idea what had been taking place here. A few days ago, he had forgotten his camera in the hanger while parking his heptr. When he remembered today, that he had kept it in a room on the mezzanine floor, he had rushed in, afraid that the LTTE operatives or someone else might have taken it.

He was still checking the camera bag when he heard a man speaking with authority in Sinhalese in the hanger hall below, and an interpreter translating it into Tamil. He looked outside the room and saw the LTTE operatives surrounded by SLAF commandoes pointing their weapons at them.

There was a Brigadier rank officer, who Prakash recognised as the Brigade Commander of the SLAF deployed at Jaffna.

'You are now in the custody of the SLAF', said the interpreter, translating what the Brigadier was saying.

'Do not fear us, we will look after you', he said. 'In a few moments, we will transport you by plane to Colombo.'

Prakash was on his knees now, his body shaking out of control. He was scared of being spotted and misconstrued as a spy. He wanted to get away from here, but the only way out was through the huge sliding doors that were partially open and guarded by the SLAF. Prakash could see ambulances and military jeeps parked outside the building, an outer cordon of the SLAF commandoes. He looked around frantically and desperately for his own Para Commandoes, but was petrified when he could not see them around.

There was some commotion in the hall below. The LTTE operatives were now sitting in three circles of six, hands raised sideways with open palms, rotating their hand clockwise and anti-clockwise alternatively.

Pulendran stood up and said something in Tamil to the Brigadier.

'They will not go to Colombo because you will torture them to say what you want them to say in front of the media', the interpreter said to the Brigadier.

'How the f**k do they know that? Tell them we will not do anything of this sort', the Brigadier told the interpreter and gestured to the LTTE operatives to indicate a no.

'We know you well. For hundreds of years, what have you given us? Poverty, deprivation, torture, murder, rape, and destruction. You will not give us anything more now', Pulendran said.

He raised his hands and turned toward the other LTTE operatives. It was then that Prakash saw them pulling out the cyanide capsule from inside their shirt. He had been unable to see it around their necks as the SLAF standing around them had blocked his vision.

The SLAF had no idea that cyanide capsules had gone in with the *sapadh*.

'*Tamil Elanukku*', for the Tamil Eelam, Pulendran shouted as if it were a battle cry.

All the others repeated the war cry, and before the interpreter could translate, or the Brigadier and the SLAF commandoes could react, the LTTE operatives took the cyanide capsule and bit into it. They lay down flat on the floor to let the cyanide enter their bloodstream and react faster.

'Cyanide, cyanide!', shouted the Colonel of the SLAF commandoes.

Pulendran and Kumar died instantaneously as they had consumed two capsules each.

The commandoes rushed towards the LTTE operatives and started kicking them in the stomach to make them vomit the cyanide. Some stretcher-bearers came rushing in, put the operatives on the stretchers, and moved them to the ambulances. Sirens blaring, the ambulances started leaving the hangar area.

Normally, cyanide could take two to five minutes to kill a person, but the deadly combination with the acid made it enter the bloodstream within seconds. The LTTE operatives were already frothing and unconscious within thirty-forty seconds.

Pulendran was dead before he had hit the floor hard; his head was bleeding.

The Brigadier was shouting orders, but in this melee, no one was listening or following them.

Prakash was still frozen in his concealed position, and he did not dare move, fearing that he might be taken as an eyewitness to what happened.

In a few moments, the hanger was clear of all the SLAF personnel and Prakash slowly crawled out of his hiding spot and walked out of the building. He was trembling like an adolescent who had just had his first brush with sex. He was panting as he walked fast towards his room in the next building.

The scene in the airforce hospital at the Palaly Airfield was chaotic. The LTTE operatives were either unconscious or dead by the time they reached the emergency room of the hospital.

Pulendran's heart went into seizure within seconds of consuming the cyanide capsules and he had been brought in dead, said the young doctor. He could not do much to revive him. Kumar did not stand a chance either.

The Colonel was shouting at the doctor, 'Get this one to survive', he said, pointing towards Pulendran.

But Pulendran, along with Kumar, was already dead,

with froth and blood still seeping from his open mouth.

The others were also in various stages of death; dead or nearly dead and dying.

With the amount of cyanide inside them, it would be a miracle if they avoided death, thought the doctor.

Four of the eighteen survived, not because of any medical miracle but because they had only consumed half the ampule and the SLAF soldiers had kicked them real hard, which had resulted in them vomiting out whatever had gone in. The rest was done by the saline water that the medical team pumped inside their stomach.

The bodies of all the LTTE operatives were lined up in the corridor leading to the emergency room and handed over to the SLAF Colonel.

'This is a big f**k up, this is a big f**k up', he kept repeating as he walked up and down the corridor, unable to decide how to break the news to his seniors. He knew that like the corridor which ended on both sides, his career had also ended. He walked into the emergency room, picked up the phone, and dialled a number.

'LTTE cadres, Lt Col Pulendran and Kumarappa ingested cyanide and committed suicide, along with sixteen other cadres. The names of the dead are Major Abdullah, Captains Karan, Ragu, Palani, and Miresh, Lts Thavakumar, Anbalagan, second Lt Anandakumar, Lt Reginald, Captain

Nalan, and four others who were unidentified while in the custody at Palaly SLAF main base on 5 October 1987, around 5:05 pm. Log it', he said solemnly into the phone.

Prakash was frantic. He rushed into his room and found Bishnoi flipping through a five-year-old Playboy magazine.

'The LTTE guys consumed cyanide, f**k man, just like that. It was in their food. The ampules we let in. F**k man. They frothed like rabid dogs, and now they will all die. There is going to be chaos Bishnoi, utter f*****g chaos.' He was livid.

The wind just carried the news of the mass suicide to the world outside the Palaly airport, and by evening, all hell broke loose. Reports started pouring in from SLAF posts, that they were being targeted by the LTTE cadres all over the Jaffna peninsula. A few of the IPKF posts were also fired upon, and they were told to maintain restraint. Everyone was frantically looking for Prabhakaran.

Sheonan heard shots being fired around the airfield and came out of his tent to alert his team. He saw Ranjit and Nair standing outside, looking in the direction of the sound of fire.

'It seems we are finally going to have some action now, boss', Ranjit said, looking towards Sheonan.

'What else can you expect from the politicians, just f**kups', replied Sheonan.

'Tell your teams to be ready, just in case we have to move in for some reason. Also, be alert, you never know with these LTTE guys, they may decide to get inside the airfield. Let's be clear, we are here to support the LTTE, so if they attack the SLAF, we look the other way. Is that clear? Brief your teams accordingly', Sheonan said.

'Yeah, that's right', said Nair as Sheonan moved out of hearing range. 'Why should we get into their shit?', he asked Ranjit. Ranjit just nodded and smiled.

'It is not about whether we want to or not, we will be sucked into this mess before we even know what is happening. It is not as simple as it seems, and the game plan has been neatly laid out by the stakeholders. Unfortunately, we will only see it when it's too late', he declared, rather philosophically.

Nair gave him a puzzled look. Ranjit did speak like this once in a while, he assumed that the person listening to him knew the background and references he was making and would understand his statement.

Ranjit looked at Nair and said, 'You just wait and watch'.

DEPI MEETS ANNA

CHAPTER 4

THE MEETING THAT STARTED THE END

The meeting with Prabhakaran was going to be a sensitive issue to handle and the government needed a mature and experienced person to negotiate with him. Dixit had recommended Lt Gen Depinder 'Depi' Singh, who was the Southern Army Commander and also the Overall Force Commander (OFC). He was an officer with thirty-three years of active military service and had served as military assistant to Field Marshal SHFJ 'Sam' Manekshaw, during the 1971 Indo-Pak conflict. A highly decorated soldier from the Gorkha Regiment, he was considered a man with excellent negotiation skills.

A tall Sikh officer, Depi had done his schooling at Colonel Brown School in Dehradun. His father was the

JCO ADC to the Governor of Maharashtra, and on his retirement, he had a letter of reference from the governor for his son to be admitted to any good school in Dehradun, his town of preference to settle down.

After visiting the many schools in Dehradun, his father decided to admit him to Colonel Brown. On completion of his schooling, Depi joined the army and was commissioned into the first battalion of the fourth Gorkha regiment.

Depi and Prabhakaran shared a good rapport and had met several times, prior to and post the signing of the peace accord.

It was a unanimous decision between the military and civilian decision-makers, to send Depi to work with Prabhakaran and broker a truce with him. It could be through persuasion, negotiation, or pure coercion, Depi was given a free hand to deal with him.

On the morning of 9 October, Depi landed at the Jaffna University football ground in a Chetak helicopter, without his staff officer. He did not want any of his staff officers around while he was negotiating with Prabhakaran, he was apprehensive that things could get ugly as the latter would definitely be upset.

On landing, Depi was escorted by two LTTE cadres and was guided into a room in the University Geography department, which was now the military headquarters of the LTTE. It was a room big enough to seat forty-fifty people and had been converted into the LTTE ops room. Depi was awe-struck by the way the room was laid out, like a typical ops room of the Indian Army. Well, he thought, that is where they learnt their basics from. He saw large maps of Jaffna, with locations of the IPKF and SLAF camps and outposts marked on them, including troop levels, order of battle (ORBAT), weapon profiles, and all militarily relevant information detailed on them.

Impressive was the word that came to his mind. Gopalaswamy Mahendraraja, the second-in-command of the LTTE political wing, whose *nom de guerre* was Mahattaya, walked into the room. Depi recognised him, having met him once with Prabhakaran.

'Good morning General, please have a seat', Mahattaya said, pointing towards a chair placed opposite a single-seater sofa that was obviously meant for the one who would chair the meeting.

'The Supremo will join us in a moment', he said.

A few of the senior LTTE cadre could speak English, though highly accented.

Depi looked at him and smiled.

All the LTTE commanders had aliases to hide their true identities, and also to protect their families from the atrocities of the SLAF.

'Would you care for some coffee?', Mahattaya asked.

'No thanks.'

As if on cue, Prabhakaran and Yogarathinam 'Yogi' Jogi walked into the room.

Vellupillai Prabhakaran, *Thambi* or *Anna* as he was called by his close associates, seemed very annoyed. He sat down on the chair opposite Depi.

'General, it is rather surprising and sad that you did not help us when we needed it the most. It is because of you that we have lost fourteen of our cadres', he began.

Prabhakaran, the wily guerrilla leader that he was, was forever prepared for the moment when one or both signatories to the accord would break their sovereign word.

Mahattaya and Yogi were standing on either side of him.

All three of them were all dressed in the combat fatigues of the LTTE. It was a camouflage pattern printed on cotton, which some of them wore as a shirt and trousers, and some as a jacket instead of the shirt. Everyone wore the same uniform with not an iota of difference. Some factory in Madras was doing a real good job. In comparison, the IPKF soldiers wore at least fifty different shades and prints of the newly introduced combat uniform. Maybe he should go back and look for this factory or ask Prabhakaran about it, thought Depi.

'Mr Prabhakaran, kindly accept our sincere condolences for the loss of the fighters who consumed cyanide at the Palaly airfield. Although we wanted to help you, the accord had our hands tied', began Depi.

'This is a big personal loss to me, you know? Kumar was my brother-in-law and now I have no way to face my sister', Prabhakaran replied, rather morosely.

'Yes, I am aware. My personal condolences to you and your dear sister', Depi responded sincerely.

Then, after pausing for a few seconds, he continued, 'You are aware that both the governments want this impasse to end soon, without any confrontation between the LTTE and the IPKF. This unfortunate incident should not escalate into a confrontation between us. I suggest that it be taken as a percussor to a peaceful settlement. Let the fourteen LTTE fighters be martyrs who laid down their lives to usher in peace for the Tamil people. Let their death not go waste. Let them be honoured and remembered as freedom fighters', said Depi concluding with the hyperbole.

'It is too late to talk about peace now General', Prabhakaran said, almost in a whisper.

'If you surrender, as was decided in the accord, then we can negotiate with the GoSL to acknowledge your presence in Jaffna as a legitimate and internationally recognised government, and then you can do whatever good you want for your Tamil people', said Depi, throwing Prabhakaran the bait.

'I would rather die fighting than surrender to the IPKF or our enemies, the SLAF', Prabhakaran declared.

Depi knew that the discussion was going south and Prabhakaran was getting more adamant by the moment. 'I am sure we can find a *via media* to this impasse and reach an amicable solution', he suggested.

'Weak people find compromises that are generally lopsided and in favour of the negotiator. We do not want anything of this sort.'

'I suggest that the IPKF and the SLAF both get out of my area. Let us govern the area as we were doing before you came in', continued Prabhakaran, bluntly putting his proposal across to Depi.

'I do not think that can happen. The accord has to be respected and implemented, in letter and spirit', said Depi.

'The accord is for you and the GOSL. I have nothing to do with it because I was not a part of the agreement. No one asked me whether I agreed with it or not. I was very cleverly kept out of it by your Prime Minister and Jayewardene. I became a laughing stock among my people, but I swallowed the humiliation, thinking and believing that you meant good for the Tamils. You can ask Mahattaya and Yogi, they will tell you that there was a near rebellion among the cadre, against my decision to let the IPKF take our weapons, but I managed to convince them somehow. Now see what has happened?', Prabhakaran said, his voice rising in pitch with each sentence he spoke. He was angry, more because of the humiliation than the situation he was in now.

'I can understand your predicament but…'

'No you cannot General, you definitely cannot understand, because you are not a Tamilian who has been subjugated to hundreds of years of slavery, poverty, torture, and rampant discrimination. You will not understand the helplessness of the parents whose sons have been picked up by the SLAF, disappearing in the middle of the night, never to return to their homes. You will not understand the humiliation and agony of the young girls who have been raped, some of them murdered, by the SLAF. General, it is easy to talk when you have lived a privileged life. I will settle for nothing less than the Tamil Eelam and let that be very clear to the Government of India and the GOSL', concluded Prabhakaran.

'Mr Prabhakaran, that may not be a very wise decision', Depi said, keeping his pitch and tenor in control.

'The peace accord has to be implemented in whichever way it may be possible. We are here to make peace, and we wish to implement it amicably. I again request you to kindly consider my proposal and agree to peacefully resolve this situation', he pleaded.

'My answer is NO', Prabhakaran said in a flat voice.

'You are aware that your cadres will be no match for the mighty Indian Army. Many Tamil lives will be lost in any armed confrontation. The Government of India considers the Tamils of Sri Lanka as their friends and wants no harm to come to them. It is in this spirit that the accord was signed and will be implemented, but any armed offensive action against the IPKF will not be tolerated, and we will retaliate in self-defence. It will be an unfortunate situation but a soldier of the IPKF will fire to kill', Depi said.

'Are you trying to frighten me, General?', Prabhakaran asked.

'No, as your friend, Mr Prabhakaran, I am forewarning you so that you do not put your cadre in harm's way.'

'My dear General', said Prabhakaran, 'I will show the Indian Army what insurgency is. The world will witness the most brutal and sophisticated insurgency, here in Jaffna. I repeat, we will die, but we will not surrender'.

This was the final nail in the coffin, and Depi knew it would be fruitless to carry on the meeting any further.

'Well, you have made your decision and so be it. May god be with you. Goodbye.' Depi said, getting up and extending his hand towards Prabhakaran.

Prabhakaran got up too, shook Depi's hand warmly, and smiled.

'Do not get me wrong, General, I have a dream to achieve', he said.

Depi smiled back and walked away.

'This is the best decision you have made in your life and you will not regret it for as long as we live', said an elated Mahattaya, the moment Depi was out of earshot.

'Why do you say that?', asked Prabhakaran rather earnestly, as he respected Mahattaya's and Yogi's opinion on all issues concerning the LTTE.

'Because the Indians will never let you have what you are dreaming about. Didn't they cheat you with the accord? They said it would be a tripartite agreement and look what happened. We were made to look like fools. The Indians promised that they would not hand over our fighters to the SLAF and even after you begged them, they just withdrew from the building in which the fighters were housed and let the SLAF take them. If you had not sent the cyanide capsules, they would all be in the custody of the SLAF, in front of the media. That Dixit wants you killed, by hook or by crook. They promised you that LTTE would be the only group to negotiate with the GoSL, and all the others would be finished. What happened? They are now arming the EPRLF and the other groups against us, and they still want us to believe that they will make you the Chief Administrator of Jaffna?', Mahattaya said.

'You must also see it from the international perspective', said Yogi, who had spent many years in London and was well-versed in international affairs.

'The Khalistan movement in India is being supported by Pakistan in the same manner that India is supporting us. The Anandpur Sahib Resolution is very similar to the proposal we are making. The district of Ajnala in Punjab is in the same position that Jaffna is today. If India declares Jaffna an autonomous region without the consent of the GoSL, then Pakistan can do the same and declare Ajnala an autonomous region without the consent of the Indian Govt. Therefore, India will never declare Jaffna as an autonomous region, and neither will the GoSL. The IPKF will capture all of us and hand us over to the GoSL, who will massacre all the LTTE fighters. The Indians will, in return, ask for a permanent base in Sri Lanka which the GoSL will happily agree with in exchange for us', explained Yogi, and they saw Mahattaya nodding in agreement.

Prabhakaran remained in stunned silence.

'The general does not know what the Indian government has in mind, he is just a messenger. He was sent to convince you', Mahattaya said.

'How do you know all this? Do you have any evidence or

source or have you made this story up?', asked a concerned Prabhakaran.

'We have penetrated the core of the Indian intelligence, bureaucracy, and military. Our people are everywhere, holding positions of authority. Every single plan, decision, and minute of their meetings are known to us. Every word that Mahattaya and I have said, is from the horse's mouth. Do you know that Rajeev Gandhi addresses Jayewardene as uncle?', Yogi said, laughing.

'Yes, this is true. So then what can you expect from him, he will listen to what Jayewardene says, and not to you', said Yogi.

'That I know, which is why I did not agree to surrender. Both of you try to find out what the IPKF is planning against us so we can surprise them, instead of them surprising us', Prabhakaran said.

Depi was on the way to Palaly airport, he had known beforehand, that Prabhakaran would not agree to surrender. Now that the balloon had gone up, the IPKF would have to be ready for an armed conflict with the LTTE. This was not a situation Depi had wanted to be in, but unfortunately, had no control over it.

The heptr landed at Palaly airport, where Depi switched to a fixed-wing Avro aircraft that would take him to Madras. This was also a daily routine for him, to fly into

Sri Lanka early morning and fly out by lunchtime. In the aircraft, he would dictate the day's proceedings to his PA, who would, in turn, type it out in the flight, and hand it over to the Colonel General Staff at the ad hoc air force headquarters at Madras.

'9 October 1987, 1230 hours IST. Meeting with Prabkhakaran, Supreme Commander, LTTE at Jaffna University, Jaffna. Others present at the meeting were…', Depi started dictating the minutes of the meeting to his PA. Every minute detail was mentioned in the minutes because of its importance and criticality. Depi did not want anyone to get the impression that he had not tried hard enough to strike a deal or think that he was a General who preferred war to peace.

'… It is my assessment that the IPKF should now be ready for a prolonged and deadly armed confrontation with the LTTE, and accordingly, the force level is to be increased after detailed inter-services consultation and planning. That will be all', Depi said to his PA as the Avro started its descent into the air force airfield at Tambaram in Madras.

THE S**T HITS THE FAN

CHAPTER 5

A SURPRISE AWAITS THE SHBO

No one had realised their absence until Ranjit brought up the issue of the missing five-man team, sometime in the evening. They had gone to Jaffna early in the day to buy some groceries and get a volleyball—their only source of entertainment—repaired. Purchasing groceries and fresh vegetables was a daily chore that they had been performing since they had come to Palaly. They had left in a 1-ton and should have been back by ten or eleven o'clock, but after the suicide incident and the ensuing chaos thereafter, no one had realised that they had not returned.

'Let's wait the night out, maybe they went into one of the IPKF camps because of the situation, they may call us or return in the morning', Sheonan said, when Ranjit brought up the issue with him.

The whole night, the LTTE SAs firing around the airfield kept everyone up, fearing the possibility of an attack on their camp.

At the break of dawn on the tenth of October, with no news of the lost five-man team, Ranjit and Sheonan gathered a search patrol of twelve commandoes and moved on foot, towards the town of Jaffna. The complete detachment of the Para Commandoes had just one 1-ton and a Jonga, so they left the Jonga behind and decided to move on foot.

They walked through the neighbourhood, enquiring whether the locals had seen the men around, but they drew a blank. They walked all morning and afternoon until they reached the 54 Division Ordnance Unit (DOU), located at Jaffna. Neither the 1-ton nor the men could be found.

At the DOU, they heard of the LTTE ambushes on IPKF vehicles and resulting casualties, but still, no trace of their 1-ton. The OC of the DOU gave them two 1-tons and had them dropped back at the camp. Even at the airfield, there was no news of the missing men. They feared the worst.

Unknown to them, the 1-ton with itss five occupants had been ambushed on its way to Jaffna. All the soldiers had been killed and their bodies burnt. The bodies and weapons, and the vehicle, were never to be recovered.

The situation in Jaffna deteriorated very quickly. The bad-to-worse phase did not go the way it should have normally gone, it just started from worse, and then worsened by the hour. A large number of IPKF posts were attacked by the LTTE, foot and vehicle columns were ambushed, and soldiers were kidnapped. The transition from peace to wartime caught them unaware. None of the IPKF soldiers had been carrying weapons until these incidents started taking place.

Locally, the LTTE commanders were still on friendly terms with the IPKF, but it took minutes for them to turn hostile. The IPKF was left counting its casualties and looking for its MIA soldiers.

General Harkirat knew the LTTE cadre well by now and had already anticipated the reaction and reply of the LTTE supremo, so when Depi's minutes of his meeting with Prabhakaran reached him in the evening on the fax, he was not surprised.

He smiled at Hoshiyar, his Col GS, and said, 'Surely, this is what was meant to happen. Did you think that the LTTE would give up so easily? No way! They will fight us. They have the advantage of knowing their land and their people, and a dedicated cadre that is loyal and well-trained. But we need to get them before they can get into combat mode and take on the IPKF', he warned Hoshiyar.

'That is true Sir, but the fact remains, that we do not have the wherewithal to deal with them right now', he replied.

'One of the factors for success in any operation is surprise my dear boy, and if we can achieve surprise, then the results that a small force can achieve are manifold; more than what a larger force can achieve. I do not have to tell you that, you have been a commando throughout your life. We have to plan something in which the surprise element is the main factor of the battle', Harkirat explained.

'I know you already have a plan in your mind Sir, let's hear it', said Hoshiyar, knowing the General pretty well by now.

He and Harkirat shared a very special bond as GOC and Col GS. Hoshiyar always respected Harkirat for his bold and audacious plans that had held them in good stead during the army-level test exercises in the deserts of Rajasthan, prior to being inducted into Sri Lanka.

Harkirat found Hoshiyar to be a very meticulous and professionally-thorough officer who was always pragmatic and put his operational experience to good use.

'Yes, I do', Harkirat said, feeling rather proud of himself, before unravelling his master plan to eliminate the LTTE.

'Hoshiyar, we are sure now that the top leadership of the

LTTE, including Prabhakaran, are at the Jaffna university complex. They have established both their operational and political headquarters there. Correct?', he asked Hoshiyar.

'Correct Sir', he replied.

'Good', continued Harkirat.

'So, if we plan an operation for the capture or elimination of the LTTE top leadership at Jaffna university, we can take them completely by surprise, and in one stroke, we will be able to remove their decision-making mechanism. Which, in turn, will leave them headless, resulting in the complete breakdown of the LTTE cadre. This will shatter the organisation and they will have no desire to fight. Ultimately, they will either surrender or get annihilated', Harkirat concluded triumphantly.

Hoshiyar was a lifelong Special Forces officer and had commanded the 10 Battalion of the Parachute Regiment (Commando). Only a rookie would be taken in by Harkirat's rhetoric so easily, so he probed further, 'Sir, how do you plan to implement this?'

'We have a company of 10 Para here and we also have 13 Sikh LI moving in tomorrow, from Gwalior to Trincomalee and Vavuniya. We will take permission from the OFC to make this unit available to us for twenty-four hours, only for this operation. After which the unit will be relieved to go back to their original operational task', said a beaming Harkirat.

'Sir, in case we wish to use this unit tomorrow, then the unit will only have a few hours to prepare for the operation, and it may not be an ideal situation, to commit them to an operation without preparation and rehearsal', Hoshiyar argued.

'What's wrong with you Hoshiyar? You are a Special Forces man yourself and you want to play by the books?', Harkirat mocked Hoshiyar.

'As I said earlier, surprise is our biggest weapon, and we will use it against the LTTE. The earlier we launch, the bigger the surprise, and we will be able to capture all of them in one place, in one go. Hoshiyar, let us not allow this chance to slip away from our hands. Imagine the shock Prabhakaran will feel when he is captured, and that is when we will be able to make him agree with whatever we want. Politically, and militarily, this will be a master stroke. You do not have to think about it too much, just plan the operation. To achieve maximum surprise, plan a Special Heliborne Operation (SHBO), with the Paras leading and the Sikh LI building up on them', Harkirat finished.

'But Sir…', Hoshiyar wanted to say something.

'No buts, Hoshiyar. I have the complete plan in my head', he said, pointing to himself.

'I will discuss it with General Depi and give you the

green light. Meanwhile, get 13 Sikh LI to land at Palaly, and not Trinco and Vavuniya. I hope that is understood?'

'Yes Sir', replied Hoshiyar.

NAAM HAI TERA (13)

CHAPTER 6

THE SAGA BEGINS

'I must confess that my transfer from the 4th Battalion, The Brigade of Guards, to the 13th Battalion, The Sikh Light Infantry, had come as a rude shock to me. Twenty-two years in a regiment, and just when you were dreaming of commanding your own battalion, the army headquarters shifts you out, and not to another battalion of your regiment, but an entirely different regiment. I was depressed, angry, and disillusioned, and I remember telling my darling wife Sujata that I would resign. But she convinced me that the army is the army, and it really does not matter which regiment you are in. "You are an excellent soldier", she told me, "and your troops will like you. You will start loving them just as you love the Guardsmen".

And ladies and gentlemen, here I stand in front of you today, thanking my wife for the wonderful advice that she gave me when I was down in the dumps. I also thank all of you, my officers, your lady wives, and of course, the gallant Sheras, who in the last two years of my command of 13 Sikh LI have always made me feel proud to be your Commanding Officer. Not once have I regretted listening to my wife's advice. You all are surely and purely "Guru's Own", as the unit is known. These past two years have been very taxing on all of us as we were moved to the deserts for operational familiarisation immediately on our arrival from Ladakh. Then, on our return, we moved to Bangalore for four months, and ever since, have been in a state of flux. I hope we will now get some time to settle down and spend time with our families. Although we are still on our four-hour notice and can be inducted into a whole new role at a new place, with the situation as it is, it may take a moment to go from stand by to stand down. This dinner party tonight is to celebrate these two years of a wonderful command that I have had, and I hope and pray that we grow from strength to strength, and that the *kripa* of the Guru, remains on us. Thank you.'

'*Jo bole so nihaal*', he called out the Sikh's religious *Jaikara*, '*Sat sri akal*', shouted all those present at the venue.

Lieutenant Colonel Randheer Shamsher 'Bubbles'

Sethi stepped down from the small stage that had been temporarily erected for this party, as the unit's six-piece jazz band, made up entirely of soldiers, started to play *Congratulations and celebrations*. It did not matter if the song went with the occasion or not, just as long as it had the words congratulations and celebrations in it. There was thunderous applause from all the officers and their wives as Bubbles went around shaking hands and receiving cheers and, in turn, thanking all of them. His wife walked along, beaming and thanking everyone as well.

A man of medium build, Bubbles sported a bushy moustache that curled upwards. He had taken over the unit just three years after its conception, and over the next two years of his command, he had made sure that the unit had an SOP for nearly every activity. They trained hard and partied harder. His command approach was very humane, although he never spared them for even an iota of indiscipline. He was revered more than he was feared. A graduate of the prestigious Staff College, his career had been on the fast track until now.

'It was nice of you to have thanked everyone', Sujata had told Bubbles as he stepped down from the stage. He had smiled at her.

Captain Birender 'Biru' Singh walked up to Bubbles, escorted by a waiter with a drink.

'Your poison, Sir', he said, offering Bubbles the drink.

'Thank you Biru, actually, I should be offering you the drink', Bubbles said apologetically.

'Where are your wife and the newborn angel?', asked Sujata.

'I will go get them, they are in the kid's room', replied Biru.

'Don't you have a maid to look after all the kids here?', asked Bubbles, looking towards Sujata.

'Yes we do Bubbles, but there are some things that only a mother can do', Sujata replied rather sternly. Bubbles got the hint and kept his mouth shut after that.

Bubbles and Sujata then moved among the officers and the ladies, exchanging pleasantries and making small talk. Bubbles quite liked Biru and wanted him to do well professionally. He was talking to the second-in-command (2IC) when he saw Biru walking in, this time with his wife, Bhavna. She complimented his personality excellently and Bubbles was happy for them.

'There you are', said Bubbles. 'How are you and the little angel?', he asked her.

'We are both fine, thank you', she replied, a little self-consciously.

'Now that you are here, let us have a nice song from you and Biru, like always', interrupted the 2IC.

'Yes, that is a part of every party that we have, get on the stage', Bubbles said.

'Sure Sir', Biru replied and held Bhavna's hand to lead her to the stage.

It was a nice song, one that they usually sang. Then, they requested the officers and the ladies to join them on the dance floor.

Bubbles and Sujata were also on the floor when the mess havildar walked up to Captain Shirvalkar, who was the adjutant, and passed a message to him. Shirvalkar moved to Bubbles and told him that there was a phone call from the Brigade Commander for him. Bubbles excused himself and walked into the mess phone booth.

'Hello, yes, this is CO, 13 Sikh LI', he confirmed to the telephone operator in the exchange.

'Good evening Sir, Commander 72 Brigade would like to speak to you Sir', he said.

'Sure, put him through', Bubbles replied.

Brigadier SK Mishra was Bubbles' Brigade Commander, and as a rule, never rang up any CO after office hours, unless there was an emergency. Bubbles went on alert.

Bubbles could hear some clicks, and after a few seconds of ringing, he heard the operator again, speaking to the Commander.

'Good evening Sir, your call to CO 13 Sikh LI. He is

on the line, carry on Sir', the operator said.

'Good evening Sir', said Bubbles, the moment the operator finished.

'Good evening my good man, did I catch you at a party?'

'Yes Sir, but that's alright. Just celebrating the second year of my command with my team Sir', Bubbles said.

'That's a nice gesture, I think you are doing great, keep it up Bubbles.'

'Thank you, Sir', Bubbles replied.

'So, why don't you and I have quick drink at my place, I promise I will not keep you for long. Ten minutes at the most. Just come over', Mishra said.

'I will be there in a jiffy Sir, it is always a pleasure to have a drink with you.'

He walked quickly to the lawn outside and told the 2IC to carry on with the party and that he would re-join them in ten minutes.

Bubbles jumped into his jeep and drove to the commander's residence, about 500 metres from the mess.

The commander was formally dressed in a grey flannel suit, complete with a matching tie. He was waiting on the porch to receive Bubbles.

Bubbles greeted the commander, who in turn shook hands with him and guided him to his study, which was a small room just next to the porch. The room was tastefully done in teak wood, with leather furniture to match the colour. There was a huge bookshelf that covered the entire wall opposite the door. There was a large table in the centre of the room, with a light green leather cover on it. There were two large single-seater sofas on the side, with a small bar behind them. Mishra poured two drinks into crystal-cut glasses and offered one of them to Bubbles.

'Cheers, to your command', he said, clinking the glasses.

'Cheers Sir, and thank you very much', replied Bubbles.

The official residence of the Commander had been the erstwhile residence of the Prime Minister of the Kingdom of Gwalior, and the army had managed to maintain the palace with the same grandeur and splendour.

'Well', said the commander, 'Bubbles, the time has finally come for HQ 72 Infantry Brigade and 13 Sikh LI to move to Sri Lanka, to be a part of the IPKF. You have been on stand-by for some time now and have also spent about four months in Bangalore. That, I think, will hold you in good stead in your new role. We are supposed to move tomorrow by air. The rest of your heavy loads will move by rail, and then by ship from Madras. The details will be given to you by the Brigade Major and the DQ. I will not brood on the situation in Sri Lanka as I am sure you know more about it than me', the Brigade Commander said.

They still discussed the situation in Sri Lanka for some time, and after that, the Commander wished Bubbles the best of luck while departing.

When Bubbles reached the party, it was still on with the same gusto. They did not know what lay in store for them.

'I do not want to spoil the mood', he told his second-in-command, as both of them walked into the mess building, away from music.

'Executive orders have been issued to move to Sri Lanka. Troops move by air and heavy equipment by rail. Alpha and Bravo company to Vavuniya, and the two companies, Charlie and Delta, with the Battalion headquarters. Headquarter company and the headquarters of the brigade moves to Batticaloa. The task is mainly garrison duties. Come on, let us have dinner, get the officers in, and allow the ladies to leave.'

***

'Gentlemen, we are finally moving to Sri Lanka', started Bubbles, after the ladies had left and the officers had settled down comfortably in the anteroom.

'This will be a momentous day in our history, and I want

all of you to be prepared for any eventuality, although we know that not much is happening in Sri Lanka. As part of the IPKF, our job is to implement the peace accord, which is already in place in Sri Lanka, and general amnesty has been granted to all separatist organisations in the country. We are being inducted to ensure that this surrendering of arms by the separatist organisations is done peacefully and quickly so that the provincial elections in the Jaffna Peninsula are held in time, and the elected government can take over the governance. The troops will move by air and heavy equipment by train. Therefore, you all will have to prepare two load tables. Alpha and Bravo companies move to Vavuniya and battalion less two companies with the brigade Headquarters' to Batticaloa. We have been placed directly under the command of the 54 Infantry Division which has been there for four months. We are on our four-hour notice, therefore, we need to get cracking on this now. Any questions?', he asked.

Captain Shirvalkar, who was the adjutant, asked, 'Sir, do we recall the people who are on leave, or completing courses and other duties away from the unit?'

'No. A general mobilisation has not been ordered, therefore, they will report at the embarkation headquarters at Tambaram Madras, on completion of their course, leave, or attachment. They will reach their respective company locations by routine air courier once a week. I want you to get as much information as you can on the operational situation before we leave. Best of luck and godspeed', Bubbles concluded.

'Sir, the unit is at 60 per cent strength presently, and with a rear party to be left here, and other administration detachments that will be spread from Madras onwards, we may practically just have about 45 per cent effective combat strength of soldiers on the ground', Shirvalkar had the cadre statistics on his fingertips.

'Well, maintain minimum strength here. Only those who are not allowed on the field, by virtue of their medical category. As far as the administration detachments in Madras are concerned, keep no one. The embarkation HQ there will handle everything. I repeat, for the benefit of all present here, we have no orders to recall', Bubbles replied.

It was a clear morning on 10 October 1987, and the unit, with all the equipment that was to be carried by air, was lined up in the PT ground. All the vehicles that were supposed to ferry the troops to the airfield had been lined up on the road behind them.

The news from the airfield was that the aircraft had still not arrived, and there was still some suspense as to when they would come, how many would be there, or from where they would be coming in.

Is this a joke?, Bubbles thought.

'We have been given orders to move but there is no information on the aircraft. We cannot do much except wait', Bubbles shrugged his shoulders as he expressed his frustration to his 2IC.

'Keep me posted about their arrival or any other news that you receive', he said, walking away towards his office.

It was well past evening and there was still no news about the aircraft. All the troops were still sitting on the PT ground, with their equipment now loaded onto the vehicles.

Maj Mohan, the 2IC, was in his office, when the phone on his table trilled. He picked it up on the first ring, anticipating a call from the airforce about the arrival of the aircraft.

'Hello', it was a female voice and he was confused.

'Hello, yes?', he replied.

'It's me', came the reply.

'Who me?', he asked, not recognising his wife's voice.

'What's wrong with you, it's me', the reply came again.

It was then that he recognised his wife.

'Oh, sorry, I was waiting for a call from the airforce station and that is why I got confused', he stammered back.

'Nothing new there, you never recognise my voice.'

'That's not true, I am sorry.'

'Anyway, I will not get angry with you because today

is *Karwa Chauth*, do you remember or have you forgotten that too?'

'Of course, I remember', he lied unconvincingly.

'All the ladies are meeting in the CO's house, to break their fast when the moon is sighted. You can bring all the officers to his place so that all the rituals can be completed there, after which we can have dinner together before you all leave', she suggested.

'That's a good idea but I will have to ask the CO.'

'Then please do so', his wife said.

Mohan had been married for ten years now and knew that on *Karwa Chauth*, married women, especially those in North India, observed a fast from sunrise to moonrise for the safety and longevity of their husbands. Therefore, they were very serious about following the ritual. They would only break their fast after the moon rose and they saw their husband's face through a sieve, if possible.

Mohan walked up to the CO's office and said, 'Sir, all the ladies are collecting at your house for the *Karwa Chauth* rituals. They are requesting all the officers to come over so the rituals can be done centrally, and we can also have dinner together before we leave. So can we allow the officers to take a break for about an hour Sir?'

'2IC', replied Bubbles rather sternly, 'All the men are still in the PT ground and they are not moving to their homes for similar rituals. Do you think it will be appropriate for some of the officers to go to my house for the *Karwa Chauth* rituals? No. We will all stay with the men. Is that understood?', Bubbles asked with an air of finality.

Mohan quietly withdrew to his office and informed his wife, who understood the mood of the CO.

At around 2030 hours, the message was conveyed by Shirvalkar, much to the CO's relief, that the aircraft to fly them to Sri Lanka had arrived.

The complete unit was now on its feet and ready to move. The 2IC reported to the CO, and orders were passed for the companies to move out.

As the convoy of vehicles slowly made its way through the cantonment roads, it passed in front of the CO's residence. The officer's ladies, in their finest sarees and jewellery, stood on the terrace of the house. They had their backs to the road as they awaited the moon's rise. It was only after seeing the moon and then their husbands that they would have broken their daylong fast, which, unfortunately, was not to happen today.

They all turned around on hearing the sound of the vehicles, hoping to see their husbands and at least wave at them.

They only saw the convoy slowly pass by the CO's house and disappear into the night, on its way to the airfield.

At the airfield gate, the corporal on duty stopped the Jeep and checked the IDs.

'Going for Operation Pawan Sir?', asked the Sergeant who had walked out of the guardroom to ensure the IDs were checked correctly, taking down the details of the convoy.

Shirvalkar nodded and handed over the details of the men and materials being carried, including the details of the vehicles.

'Lucky Sir, our boys there say that they are having the time of their life', the Sergeant said.

'Yeah, maybe, let see', he replied.

'Best of luck', said the Sergeant again, saluting and gesturing to the guard at the gate to open it.

'Thank you', Shirvalkar answered.

As the gates opened, Bubbles drove on.

'They seem to be in high spirits, these airforce guys. They always enjoy themselves whereever they go. It's only us who enjoy making our lives miserable', Bubbles said mockingly.

Both of them laughed.

As he turned towards the aircraft parking area, he saw the COO, Group captain AK Joshi, standing on the road and flagging him down.

Bubbles stopped the Jeep, got down, and saluted.

'Good evening Sir, nice to see you here', he said.

'Good evening, yeah, had to be here for you guys. Getting all these aircraft from all over the country was one hell of a f***ing task. But anyway, we have an assorted lot of aircraft and I hope they meet your requirements', he began.

'I hope so too Sir', said Bubbles, smiling back.

'We have a mix of crafts here for you. Instead of the earlier plan of allotting you nine AN32s and one IL76, we have five AN32s, four AN12s, and one IL76. That means you will have to re-distribute and pack your load accordingly', he concluded.

'That's great news', started Bubbles. 'Here, in the pitch-dark night, the complete unit has to unload every single package and re-configure them to fit into the aircraft that has been allotted to us. On top of that, we have a schedule to follow so we reach Sri Lanka on time. This is not only outrageous but damn funny. None of it is your fault Sir, I am sure you did your best. It is just how the armed forces function. Thanks for the early warning', Bubbles said, smiling at the group captain.

'Do not worry Bubbles, you have priority over all flights, so whenever you are ready, I will clear you for take-off.'

'That's very kind of you Sir', Bubbles acknowledged. He started the jeep, and off he went, towards the aircraft.

The company vehicles had started coming in. Captain

Shirvalkar flagged down the 2IC's Jeep and passed the CO's orders to unpack and repack according to the re-allotment of the aircraft.

The unit dismounted from the vehicles on the service track and got down to the task of redistribution of the loads.

Bubbles walked up to the few aircraft on the airfield to have a look and was surprised to find them not in the shape that he thought they would be in. There seemed to have been some modifications made to the interiors of these aircraft. He asked the sergeant standing next to the aircraft why the crafts had such little space inside them.

'Sir, we are based out of Guwahati and carry out maintenance drops at air-maintained posts in Mizoram and Nagaland, therefore these aircraft had to be modified. We received orders to move immediately and had no time to put these aircraft back to their original shape', he replied earnestly.

'We are f***ed. These aircraft are modified and cannot hold standard packing. We will have to unpack every damn item and try to fit them in the aircraft individually, and then do the lashing. So, start unpacking everything except the sealed ammunition boxes, and start loading them into the aircraft in whichever way you can. Just ensure that they are lashed properly', Bubbles said to Mohan, who had moved to stand beside him.

All the aircraft had still not arrived at the Maharajganj airfield at Gwalior.

The COO was right, thought Bubbles, these aircraft were coming in from all parts of the country, some of them from as far as the Srinagar air base in Kashmir. Most of them had no idea that they were supposed to go to Sri Lanka. They had only been briefed until the landing at Maharajganj airfield. Further operational briefings were supposed to take place here.

All in all, the situation was chaotic. The air force had no idea what lay ahead of them and neither did the army that was now busy packing, unpacking, redistributing and loading resources.

Finally, at 08:10 am on 11 October, the first of the aircraft took off from the Maharajganj airfield, heading southwest to refuel at the Tambaram Airforce base in Madras.

As per the changed plan now, the order of march was companies A and B flying in the IL76, the remaining units with the Brigade HQ, in the AN12s and 32s.

The equipment and stores filled up most of the space in the aircraft, and due to the modifications, the troops had hardly any place to sit. Knowing that the flying time was not too long, they had adjusted within the cramped space.

The Commander and Bubbles were bent over a tourist map that the Brigade headquarters staff had bought from a stationery shop in the market at Gwalior. Although Jaffna was only shown as a speck on the Sri Lanka tourist map, nonetheless, Bubbles wanted to orient himself to the geography of the area.

The aircraft started descending after about two and a half hours. Bubbles, who was sitting next to the navigator, put on the spare headsets.

'Where are we landing?', he asked the pilot on the IC.

'Tambaram Sir, Madras that is, for refuelling', the pilot replied.

'Great', Bubbles replied under his breath. 'How much time will it take?', he asked.

'Approximately two hours Sir', the pilot replied.

'So we can have a lunch break here?'

'Sure Sir, just make sure that the troops do not cross over the runway.'

'Wilco'

The crafts landed one after the other and moved into the service track for refuelling.

Bubbles climbed down from the aircraft and walked towards his 2IC's aircraft.

The troops were deplaning and moving into their company groups in an orderly fashion. Bubbles was pleased to see them in high spirits.

He saw the 2IC, Mohan, walking towards him.

'The men can have their lunch here and relax. We have a two-hour halt here for them to refuel', he told the 2IC.

'Roger Sir', he replied.

Bubbles' orderly placed a camp stool for him, and from his haversack, he pulled out a packet, put it on a plate, and gave it to him.

Bubbles thanked him but as he started to open his packed lunch a corporal walked up to him and saluted.

'Yes, Corporal, what can I do for you?', asked Bubbles, who was now in a joyful mood, the happenings of last night left far behind.

'Good afternoon Sir, there is an urgent call for you from the army headquarters at the ATC. Kindly follow me', the Corporal said.

Bubbles looked at his packed lunch and then at the Corporal who had already turned around and was ready to lead the way.

Bubbles then looked at his orderly and stood up.

'*Waapis aake khawanga* (I will have it once I return)', he said and started following the Corporal.

'*Sahab*, Army headquarter *walan da ki hai, oh te airconditioned office che beh ke khandey hai*', said his orderly, in typical Punjabi spirit.

The receiver was on hold when Bubbles entered the ATC reception on the ground floor of a tall building.

He picked up the receiver and said, 'CO 13 Sikh LI here'.

'Bubbles, good afternoon, this is Brigadier Aslam Khan, DDG, MO Directorate. How are you?'

'Good afternoon Sir. Couldn't be better', Bubbles replied.

'There is a slight change of orders for you. Your complete unit will now move to Palaly instead of two companies going to Vavuniya and Trinco. Is that understood?', Brigadier Aslam asked Bubbles.

'Loud and clear Sir. 13 Sikh LI will now move to Palaly Airfield', Bubbles replied, sarcasm dripping from every word he spoke.

'Come on Bubbles, cheer up, after all, you are going to Sri Lanka', Brigadier Aslam said.

'Sir, everyone seems to be envying our move to Sri Lanka but you are aware, Sir, that Lanka or Sri Lanka has never been peaceful for us, right from the days of Lord Rama. I hope history does not repeat itself.'

'Kindly inform your Commander too. You will also be getting these orders in writing in a few minutes on the telex at the ATC. Good luck', Brigadier Aslam finished.

Bubbles walked out of the ATC building, holding the

telex printout meant for his Commander. He knew that the Commander would not be a happy man on receiving these updated orders.

He whistled the tune to the *Colonel Bogey march* as he walked. It was a great stress buster for him. He always thought, 'How bad could the situation be? As bad as the prisoners in the Hollywood film, *The Bridge on the River Kwai*? If they could whistle under those harsh and inhuman circumstances, then he was certainly in a better position at the moment.

The 2IC instantaneously knew that things were not good when he saw the CO walking toward him. He had just finished eating his packed lunch and longed for a cigarette.

Before Bubbles could say something, the 2IC said, 'Sir, the pilot just informed me that the IL76 has been diverted to the Agra Airforce base due to some technical fault in the nose wheel and it will take some time for it to be operational'.

'That's great news. Kindly give this to the Commander. Tell him that I also spoke to the DDG MO Directorate on this', he said, handing over the telex to the 2IC.

Bubbles kept whistling and walked towards where his orderly was waiting for him with the packed lunch.

It was not until 3:30 pm that the first of the aircraft

landed at Palaly airport.

The first aircraft, carrying the Brigade Headquarters, the battalion HQ, and part of the support company landed and taxied towards the service track.

Bubbles stepped out of the aircraft, only to be greeted by a heavy downpour of torrential rains.

Through the rain, he could see a jeep moving towards him from the service track.

A young captain jumped out of it as it came to a halt next to the aircraft.

'Good afternoon Sir, and welcome to Sri Lanka', he said rather gleefully.

'Good afternoon', replied Bubbles and walked into the rain to the waiting jeep.

The captain introduced himself as Captain Mohit Chauhan, the General Staff Officer (grade 3, GSO3) (Int) of HQ 54 Infantry Division, which was headquartered at Palaly airfield.

'I hope you had a comfortable flight Sir', he said as they drove off to the headquarters, making conversation with Bubbles.

'Of course, it was wonderful, I was flying business class', he replied rather sarcastically.

They drove for about five minutes and reached the makeshift headquarters of 54 Inf Div. The headquarters was in a cluster of tents set up in a walled area, with about five acres of land around it. They entered the driveway, which took them between two sprawling lawns on both sides. As the jeep halted in front of the tents, Bubbles could read the plaque on a small building nearby, '1863' signifying the year of construction.

A Colonel in a maroon beret, wearing the uniform of the Commando parachute regiment, a 'Balidan' badge on his right pocket, walked out to greet him.

'Welcome Bubbles, I am Colonel Hoshiyar Singh, the Colonel GS. I have been here for ten months now, right after my Higher Command course', he said.

'The GOC, Major General Harkirat Singh, will join us in a while, he is enjoying his afternoon siesta', continued Hoshiyar winking at Bubbles.

Once inside, seated across his table Hoshiyar said, 'Well Bubbles, we have a small task for your unit tonight'.

'Let that come too, Sir', replied Bubbles.

'But before I tell you about the task, let me give you a brief update on the situation in Sri Lanka, and more specifically in the Jaffna Peninsula', he started.

'You know about the peace accord between India and Sri Lanka. It is evident that the accord has failed. As a matter of fact, it is in pieces. The LTTE had more or less weaned away from India, although the R&AW is desperately trying to keep them in its folds. If you know the R&AW, you will know that they generally do less and say more. Until now, certain weak separatist groups were being reorganised, trained, and armed, with an aim to create a counterbalancing force against the LTTE. Of course, the groups were no match for them, but they did act as a reminder to the LTTE, that they could be sidelined in this separatist movement in Sri Lanka. The LTTE realised that when the time came for negotiations, they might not be invited to sit at the negotiating table. Therefore, slowly but surely, Prabhakaran eliminated any threat to his dominance, within his organisation or outside it. The R&AW is unaware that it has raised Frankenstein's monster who, true to his character, has now gone rogue and turned against the Indian Army. R&AW is losing its grip on the LTTE if it has not already lost it. Mr Jayewardene has drafted the peace accord to his country's advantage very well, by adding a peace operating clause. Which I will read out to you for your knowledge', he said and opened a file lying on his table.

Bubbles knew about the operating clause but kept quiet.

'Para 2.16. part c, "In the event that the Government of Sri Lanka requests the Government of India to afford military assistance to implement these proposals, the

Government of India will cooperate by giving, to the Government of Sri Lanka, such military assistance as and when requested"', Hoshiyar read.

'So, this clause guaranteed that India's role was both of an instigator, in forcing the agreement forward, and of a guarantor, by deploying Indian troops as peacekeepers. This was done within forty-eight hours of signing the accord. The SLAF must have laughed all the way to their barracks. The IPKF was formed in July, and slowly and steadily, the number of troops from a mere 3000, increased to 10,000 in three months. It is getting more and more difficult to implement the accord peacefully. The LTTE is reluctant to surrender their arms and has, at certain locations, violated the peace accord, by confronting the IPKF.'

'Is the SLAF not providing any assistance to us, Sir?', asked Bubbles.

'None. They are in their barracks, having fun watching us get rogered, and they say this is just the beginning', Hoshiyar replied.

'How has the situation been after the suicide of those LTTE fighters?'

'Well, it has been getting worse by the hour, to say the least. They have started firing at our posts, all communications have been severed, and I fear that the retaliation will be an armed confrontation, so we have to be ready for the long haul. But', he paused, 'the GOC has a plan', he said.

'Bubbles, your unit, along with a company of 10 Para, has a very strategic and important mission tonight', declared Hoshiyar.

'Sir, with all due respect, I wish to state that the complete unit has still not arrived. The IL, which has two companies, developed a snag and is at the Agra airfield undergoing repairs and we do not know how long that is going to take. Secondly, it may not be a good operational decision to commit us to an operation of this magnitude within hours of landing in a terrain that is alien to us, and thirdly…'

'Come on, Bubbles', Hoshiyar said, cutting him short, 'This is not a major operation that requires days of preparation. Just take it in your stride. Do not get too stressed over it. Give me your best company commander and a company to go along with the Paras to secure the DZ; the rest of the unit can be built up', Hoshiyar said, unconcerned.

'But Sir…'

'No buts', Hoshiyar interrupted, stopping Bubbles from pleading his case.

'We will meet again in thirty minutes, in the ops room for the briefing. You will attend it with your company commander. The operation has been planned to launched tonight', Hoshiyar concluded.

'Roger Sir', Bubbles said reluctantly.

He walked out of the Div HQ and started whistling the tune of the *Colonel Bogey march*. There was nothing he could do to convince the Col GS.

The two other aircraft had landed by the time Bubbles reached the runway. He still could not see the IL76.

The weather had not relented, and it was pouring from heaven and hell.

'Rakesh (Mohan), which are the companies that have landed?', He asked the 2IC the moment he reached the runway where the troops were unloading the equipment and ammunition.

'Sir Charlie and Delta have both landed. Alpha and Bravo are on the way. They took off from Agra about an hour ago as per the ATC', he added.

'Fine. The Div HQ has planned an operation tonight. One company has to be made available for a Special Heliborne Operation (SHBO). They will operate with 10 Para. The briefing will take place in thirty minutes.'

Before Rakesh opened his mouth to say something, Bubbles continued, 'Yes, I told them that we have just landed and we need to orient, but all my requests have been shot down.'

Rakesh, who had opened his mouth to say something, slowly closed it. He had received the answer to his unasked question.

'So, nominate Charlie company to go on this mission, and tell Captain Srichand to quickly join me for the briefing', Bubbles instructed.

'Yes Sir', Rakesh replied.

'Wait, I can see Sri and Biru coming this way', Bubbles said and gave them the military field signal to come to him, touching the centre of his head with his right hand.

As it was still raining, all of them entered a small shed that was probably meant for the ORP pilot.

'So, have you managed to unload your stuff and have it organised in some way?', asked Bubbles.

'Not really Sir', said Major Birender 'Biru' Singh, 'It has been raining since we landed Sir, and after all the packing and unpacking that we had done at Gwalior, the loads are all in chaos. Although we have unloaded everything, it will take a while to get them in some order Sir.'

'Ditto Sir', said Sri, as if taking the cue and going ahead.

'The boys have been up now for more than twenty-four hours and that is taking a toll on them. Then this rain adds to the chaos. Charlie and Delta's loads are also mixed up because some of our packs did not fit into our own aircraft. As Biru Sir said, it will take a while to sort out', he explained.

'I am afraid you may not have the luxury of sorting things out at your pace. Charlie Company, under you Sri, will go on an SHBO mission with 10 Para tonight. The details will be provided to us in the briefing in the next fifteen minutes', Bubbles said.

Like Rakesh, Sri also opened his mouth to protest.

'…and I have already registered my protest but it has been shot down, so remain calm', said Bubbles, again preempting Sri's question.

'Sir, if I may say something…', Biru spoke up.

'If you are going to say that we need time for preparation etc. etc. then I am sorry to have to stop you right there. Anything else, you may ask', Bubbles said.

'Sir, I have been trained in SHBO during my tenure with my previous unit. You are aware that it is a specialised training routine that Sri has not taken. Actually, none of our boys are trained in executing SHBO missions, so it will be more appropriate to send me and Delta company, rather than Sri and Charlie', Biru finished sincerely.

Bubbles looked at Rakesh.

'I think that will be better Sir. Our troops are not trained on SHBOs, and by sending Biru and Delta, at least we will have an officer who is trained, so he can guide his men better', Rakesh said in support of Biru's statement.

'Well, then let Biru go with Delta. Any objections to

that Sri?', Bubbles asked.

'No Sir, as you wish. Your wish is our command', he added jokingly.

They all laughed.

Bubbles and Biru then left for the Div HQ. On the way, Biru stopped and informed his Senior JCO Subedar Sampuran Singh about the impending operation and instructed him to prepare accordingly.

Birender Singh Chauhan, Biru as he was known, was the scion of the erstwhile royal family of Bharatpur, but that royalty had disappeared with the Britishers a long time ago. The only thing left was an annual sports and cultural event in the village, which Biru would make a point to attend no matter where he was stationed. The army had been kind enough to grant him leave every year, during that time. He would participate in two sports—volleyball and tug-of-war. The feel of the volleyball when he smashed it gave him a sort of animal thrill. Tug-of-war, on the other hand, required raw energy and synchronisation between the team, to pull, leave, and heave. It was proof of their strength and endurance; a preparation for war. The Chauhans of Bharatpur believed that this sport had been popular even in the days of the Maharajas, a century ago. It was a man's game played by real men. As the years went by, other traditional games like sword fighting, archery, and horse riding had been cancelled for want of players and due to the difficulty of securing permissions from the police and animal rights organisations. Only tug-of-war remained of the traditional games, while the others had been replaced by volleyball, kabbadi, and last year, they had added in hockey too, but with no takers this year, it was dropped. Fourteen villages in the district still participated, even to this day. Biru was filled with pride when he saw this, the spirit had not died although the funds were drying up and the villages no longer contributed the way they used to.

The governance of the villages had been left to the Panchayats, and they were not as keen about this event as their ancestors used to be. Petty politics had reduced the games to just four, and the participating teams from thirty-six to fourteen. But Biru's enthusiasm over the years had not faded even a shade from when he had first participated with his father in 1968 when he was just twelve years.

Although not very tall, Biru was athletic and very quick on his feet. He had a mind of a military thinker and leader. It just came to him naturally, perhaps from his genes, but he was not as ruthless as his father. He had seen his father behaving like a tyrant even years after his kingdom had been dissolved, when, following the Independence of India, he had decided to join the Indian state in exchange for the benefits of the privy purse. This particular fairytale also ended when the then Prime Minister Indira Gandhi introduced the twenty-sixth amendment to the Constitution of India in July 1971, abolishing privy purses and the recognition granted to the rulers of Indian states. The Privy purses, in proportion to the size of the revenue of former princely states, had been granted to the royals at the time of Independence. It was a quid pro quo for the surrender of their ruling powers and the dissolution of their states.

The sudden transition was traumatic for his father. He never really recovered from it and suffered a massive heart attack in 1973. At just seventeen years of age, Biru was coronated as the Maharaja of Bharatpur, which really meant just a title that he could not use beyond the four walls of his palace. Biru was a conservative man when it came to royalty, title, and self-importance. He wanted to get away from all this and do something that would give him a sense of achievement and self-pride. He knew instantly that he was made for the army. He was a soldier by heart, mind, and body. Having finished his schooling at the prestigious Scindia School in Gwalior, he then went on to graduate from St Stephens in Delhi University. His mother was overwhelmed with emotional pride, that her son had followed the educational footsteps of his father, graduating in English Honours from the same college. But all hell broke loose when he announced, rather dramatically, on his return to the palace, that he had decided to join the Indian Army as an officer. The family collectively mourned the news. It spread through the district like wildfire, 'The scion of the great Chauhan clan was joining the Indian Army as a commoner'; it was a sign of the royalty going bankrupt they said. A few thought it was befitting for a Chauhan to be an officer in the Indian Army. A Rajput's duty was to defend the honour of his kingdom, which now meant India.

Maharaja Birender Singh Chauhan, as the villagers called him, shunned his title and all that went along with it, and joined the Officer's Training School in September 1975, with a promise to his mother that he would only serve for five years as a short service commissioned officer, and then come back home to look after the ancestral real estates. With no siblings, he was the natural heir to all his ancestral property.

The army never let him know where those initial five years went. Military courses to upskill himself and various other exercises kept him on his toes all the time. Being a keen sportsman, he found himself in a regiment that revered sportsmen, investing his time in playing volleyball, hockey, or basketball when he was not busy with his professional duties. He excelled in whatever he lay his hand on. In all the military courses he attended, he was either titled the best student or at least achieved a distinction. On completion of his mandatory five-year tour of duty, he was given the option to leave or continue in service. He had no doubt in his mind that he would now opt for a permanent commission in the army, going against the wishes of his mother and the people of Bharatpur, who wanted him back.

It was the thrill of the unknown and the opportunity to go beyond his physical and mental limits that Biru really loved about the army. 'Living on the edge' is how he summed it all up.

Brigadier Mishra was already in the Ops room of the Div HQ when Bubbles and Biru entered.

Hoshiyar introduced them to all the others in the room. Major Sheonan Singh and Maj Nair, who were the 2IC and the company commander of the Para company respectively, Wing commander Sapre, the heptrs Task Force commander and Flying officer V Prakash, one of the pilots, and the GSO3 whom they had already met.

Biru and Sheonan recognised each other instantaneously and shook hands.

'Nice to see you here, Sir', Biru said.

'Yes, you too', Sheonan replied.

'Gentlemen', began Hoshiyar after all of them had

settled down, 'We have definite intel that Prabhakaran, the supreme commander of the LTTE, along with his top commanders, is presently at his tactical headquarters at Jaffna university. You all are aware that after the LTTE prisoners consumed cyanide and died here on 5 October and that the peace accord is now more or less in pieces. Over the last five days, the LTTE has violated all that has been given in the accord and has promised to mount an all-out offensive against the IPKF. The Army Commander, who met Prabhakaran on the ninth, has agreed to our GOC's plan that if we capture and destroy the tactical and political HQs of the LTTE, in one strike we will be able to eliminate their top hierarchy, and with a headless LTTE, the organisation will self-destruct. Any questions so far?', he asked.

'What is the authenticity of the intel Sir?', asked Biru.

'As I said earlier, the Army Commander himself flew to meet Prabhakaran at the university in order to convince him to surrender, but he refused. As a matter of fact, he had the cheek to threaten him and tell him that he would rather die fighting than surrender', Hoshiyar replied.

'What if they have already vacated the area?'

'We have been monitoring their radio traffic and even local intelligence reports suggest that they are still in the university', Hoshiyar replied.

'Maybe they are monitoring ours too. You know Sir, they have the best communication equipment in the world. They just buy it off the shelf', Biru added.

'Biru, I know you have done your homework well, but give me some credit too. We have been in Sri Lanka for the last three months.'

Bubbles looked at Biru as if to encourage him to clear his mind before being launched into the operation.

'Well, the mission is as follows', Hoshiyar proceeded.

'Company 10 Para is to provide a firm base to 13 Sikh LI, less two companies to capture the Military Headquarters of LTTE at Jaffna University, in conjunction with one team of 10 Para by first light 12 Oct 1987.'

'The plan', he continued, 'Pathfinders ex 10 Para to take off at 2230 hours today—11 October 1987 – and secure the LZ. Air effort allotted – two MI8s. This will be followed by five MI8s for the balance of the company of 10 Para, who will also provide the firm base for 13 Sikh LI less two companies. Delta company ex 13 Sikh LI, in five MI8s, to land at the designated helipad and relieve 10 Para. Company 10 Para to capture political headquarters of the LTTE. Battalion Headquarters and Charlie company 13 Sikh LI to land and then 13 Sikh LI minus two companies to capture the military headquarters of LTTE. The complete complement of 13 Sikh LI plus 10 Para is to be ferried in seventeen sorties. Tac headquarters 72 Infantry Brigade and 5th Battalion of the 4th Gorkha Rifles (5/4 GR), now allotted to 72 Infantry Brigade, are to link up on the ground with 13 Sikh LI minus two companies and Company 10 Para, by first light on 12 October 1987. H-hour will be 0130 hours', Hoshiyar paused.

'We are aware that 13 Sikh LI has not been trained on slithering from heptrs, therefore, we have ruled that out and the heptrs will land and unload. I hope that is understood by the Air Force task force commander', he said, looking towards Wing commander Sapre.

'Understood, Sir', Sapre replied.

'Any doubts gentlemen?', Hoshiyar asked his audience.

Sheonan raised his hand.

'Yes Sheonan, I was waiting for this, shoot', Hoshiyar said jokingly.

'Sir, three points. Firstly, my pathfinders will be slithering onto the drop zone (DZ) and not landing or dismounting. It is the first element going in and I do not want to risk the enemy taking us by surprise. Landing and take-off will take time and we become vulnerable to enemy fire on the ground. Secondly, will the MI8 gunships here provide us with cover fire, or some kind of supporting fire when we go in? Lastly, do we know the exact location of the political headquarters of the LTTE?', Sheonan asked.

'Sapre', asked Hoshiyar, 'will you have a problem in case the pathfinders slither down?'

'Not at all Sir, as a matter of fact, we will be all too happy to hover and drop rather than land and unload, you know that Sir', Sapre replied.

Hoshiyar wanted to make sure that every nitty-gritty detail of the plan was clear to both the ground and air commanders.

'The second point, the MI8 gunships will not be used for this operation because we do not anticipate that kind of resistance from the LTTE, and we do not have the clearance to use heavy weapons. Lastly, do we know the location of the political headquarters of the LTTE? Well, the answer is no. We do not know the exact location, so for you, this is a seek-and-destroy mission. And that is exactly why you are going in. The best of the best', Hoshiyar said.

Sheonan smiled.

'Sir', said Bubbles, 'At the risk of repeating myself, I would like to say that I have only 320 men, all-inclusive of officers, JCOs, and the others, that is if the other two companies land in time for the mission. So when you say Bn HQ and two companies, you are really referring to about 120 men. This means I will practically have no one to reinforce the team in case it is required or anyone to link up with. Secondly, the unit has just landed, and we are still in the process of getting our equipment and stores organised. The troops have not had a hot meal since yesterday. Preparation to go in for an operation of this magnitude requires time for reconnaissance, rehearsals, and coordination. I request that the operation be postponed by at least twenty-four hours so that all necessary preparations can be made.'

'Bubbles…', but before Hoshiyar could speak any further, the GOC entered the ops room.

The GOC was of medium height, slim with greying hair; a good-looking man. His otherwise fair complexion had bronzed in the Sri Lankan sun. For an army officer, he had fairly long hair falling to his uniform shirt collar. He walked upright, with purpose and enthusiasm in his stride. He was immaculately dressed, wearing the combat uniform, along with the blood-red silk scarf of his regiment, and long, black leather boots. There was a smirk on his face.

'Gentlemen', he began, in a soft voice that betrayed his personality, 'A few of you know me', he said, looking towards Bubbles. Harkirat belonged to Bubbles' former regiment, the regiment of the Guards. Although they had not served together, his reputation in the regiment was well known. They were all known as the Guardsmen and the regiment was one of the oldest in the Indian Army. Harkirat had a deep connection with the regiment as his brother, Maj Gen

Shamsher, had commanded eight Guards during the 1971 Indo-Pak conflict with confidence, which won his unit the Battle Honour-Hilli.

'For the few who do not, let me introduce myself. I am Major General Harkirat Singh, General Officer Commanding 54 Infantry Division', he stressed and stretched the words deliberately, not using the common acronym, GOC.

'We have been here for five months now and it can safely be assumed that we know what we are talking about. Let us not come up with sissy points and suggestions on why the operation cannot be executed. FYI, this mission is the precursor to the capture of Jaffna. It has been personally planned by me and has the approval of the OFC, that is, the Army Commander. Still, in case you have any points to make, you may', he said.

'Sir', began Bubbles, 'I am Lt Col RS Sethi, CO, 13 Sikh LI'.

'Oh, come on, I know you Bubbles', laughed Harkirat. 'Get to the point'.

'I wish to put on record that the unit has landed today afternoon, and the last aircraft just about thirty minutes ago. We are still in the process of unloading and sorting out our loads as the aircraft allotted to us were not according to the load tables and we had to do a lot of repacking and loading. In addition, one of the aircraft, the IL76, was diverted to Agra for repair and has just landed. The torrential rain has further put everything in disarray. For a mission of this magnitude, I will need another twenty-four hours to recce, coordinate, rehearse, and prepare. I would request you to postpone the mission by twenty-four hours', Bubbles concluded.

'Thank you, Bubbles. I have heard you loud and clear. Let me make it clear to you, and to all you gentlemen sitting here, that the mission will go on as per the plan shared by the Col GS. No ifs and buts. Come on, you are going against a rag-tag separatist outfit that has been trained and equipped by the R&AW, and you know what the R&AW is all about. So what are you scared of? Is the mighty Indian Army getting bogged down before it even goes into combat? What the hell am I going to tell the OFC?', Harkirat was nearly shouting now.

There was pin drop silence in the room.

'We are taught never to underestimate the enemy Sir', Biru said, standing up from his seat and breaking the silence.

'Don't you f***ing teach me about Sun Tzu. I have been an instructor at the Army War College and I know better. Sit down', he commanded.

The GOC was visibly irritated, and his ego blinded

him from acknowledging the tactical facts.

'Okay, let me tell you a fact gentlemen, we do not expect any resistance from the LTTE. To make you privy to a briefing at the PMO, the Chief of R&AW, Mr Verma, has told the PM that the LTTE are "Our Boys", and they will surrender and not put up a fight. So do not get stressed about this mission. Just go and finish it. No heavy weapons are needed. The ground forces will link up at first light, so even administratively, the air compliment just needs to carry some emergency rations. The point that I am trying to make, is be as light as possible', Harkirat continued.

'The other important thing is that we do not have the maps of that area. Without recce or maps, it will be like finding a needle in the haystack', Bubbles said, when everyone else thought that the briefing had finished.

'We do not have them either', replied Harkirat, 'and my personal experience is that when you are landing on the target, you do not need maps. Come on Bubbles, do not go into irrelevant details. This is something big and I am giving it to you and your unit on a platter. It is a once-in-a-lifetime opportunity to have your name written in golden letters, in the annals of Indian Military history. This operation will be taught in military schools of instruction, as a successful model anti-terrorist operation that achieved complete surprise', he said with an air of finality.

Bubbles knew that Harkirat was getting hyperbolic and did not want to continue the discussion. He knew that Harkirat was more flamboyant than professional, and that he strongly believed in dramatizing situations to make operational tasks seem easy and uncomplicated, whereas such missions actually required immense detailing and coordination. This dominance of manipulation over morality only produced illusory gains.

Military discipline got the better of all of them and silence prevailed for the rest of the session, where the Col GS told them that a recce flight had been planned to take off right away, to show Biru and Sheonan the target area. Sapre had arranged for a Chetak heptr to fly them to a point from where they could see the same football ground of the university, where the OFC had landed earlier.

THE OPERATION

CHAPTER 7

THEY FOUGHT LIKE TIGERS

'Biru, tell the 2IC about the mission and plan on your way to the recce heptr. I will go straight to the base ops and meet the COO to coordinate further. Also, pass the initial orders to your company', Bubbles instructed.

'Wilco Sir', Biru said, acknowledging the instructions.

Biru walked briskly to reach his company. They were still trying to get their things together.

'Sahab, get the company ready to go on a mission tonight. It is an SHBO, so no heavy loads. Ground forces will link up by first light tomorrow, so load accordingly. The complete first-line ammunition will go. I am going on recce and will brief everyone in detail on return, is that understood?', Biru asked in Punjabi.

'Yes, Sir', Sampuran replied.

Biru then walked over to the 2IC. He could hear Sampuran passing on his instructions to the company, shouting at top of his voice.

Biru quickly briefed the 2IC and left for the heptr parked on the service track opposite him.

Bubbles was satisfied by the coordination with the airforce as he left the base ops after meeting the COO. The professionalism of the airforce always impressed him. He was now feeling a wee bit more confident, although his intuition told him that there were too many unpluggable holes in the plan.

He heard the *thud thud* of the Chetak heptr as he stepped out of the base ops. It was already twilight and he was not sure about the benefits of this recce.

The pilots had been instructed not to go too close to the university campus lest it compromise the secrecy and surprise of the plan. So, they flew for three minutes and then the pilot pointed ahead, to his right, and said into the headphones, 'That is the university campus, and you can also see the football ground in the centre'.

Biru could see the university buildings and the ground, although in the fading light, no other details were visible.

He estimated that the target area was approximately 3 kilometres from where they were and spread over an area of at least 3 acres. The building was a double-storied structure with a large number of rooms on both floors. Other similar buildings and single-storied structures could also be seen around the target building. The football ground was across the road, in front of it. The area around the university campus was densely populated, with a large number of houses and buildings. Lanes and by-lanes formed a web around the area. Some of the houses in the coconut and tobacco plantations were mostly shack-like structures with brick walls and a small boundary wall around them, meant more to mark their territory than to keep people away. The other houses in the area were well-constructed, with sloping roofs and structures made of fire bricks.

He looked at Sheonan who was also very intently assessing the ground details.

Before he could ask him for his opinion, the heptr turned to return.

Unknown to the occupants of the heptr, they were being watched by the LTTE fighters from a well-concealed observation post, on top of the university building. One of the LTTE fighters ran down the steps of the building and entered the room where Yogi and Mahattaya were engaged in an intimate discussion.

'Your assessment was correct Sir', he said addressing Mahattaya, 'A heptr came till about 3 kilometres of our position, hovered for a while, and then turned back', he reported.

'Good, you may go back now, and keep a close watch, okay?', Mahattaya instructed the fighter.

'So, our intercept report was correct. The battle procedure has started', Yogi said.

'Yes, a new unit has landed today afternoon and we had assessed that they would want to launch either tonight or tomorrow, to maintain the element of surprise.'

'The increase in radio traffic and the transmissions that we have intercepted clearly show that the operation will be launched tonight. The transmission between HQ 54 Infantry Division and the IPKF HQ in Madras talks of an SHBO tonight around 2230 hours', Yogi said.

'So, what are we waiting for? Let us inform *anna* and get our fighters mobilised for the start of this war against the IPKF', Mahattaya declared triumphantly.

Frantic preparations were on when Bubbles reached the runway. Thankfully, it had not rained again since they had landed, but that rain had been enough to drench all the men, their equipment, and the stores. He saw Biru briefing his company. He walked up to them. Biru halted his briefing and called the company to attend.

'Attention', he commanded.

'Dagger company, one officer, two JCOs, and forty-five

other ranks are ready for the mission Sir', he reported to Bubbles.

Bubbles was filled with pride and admiration for the soldiers who, in such a short time and under such adverse conditions, had completed their preparations for the mission.

'At ease', Bubbles said, 'I am sure that your company commander has briefed you in detail about the impending task. I am also aware that we have not received enough time to prepare adequately for it. But this is what we have always been training for and this is what I have been telling you all, that there will be a time when you will be abruptly woken up and told that you have to go on a mission. There will be no time to prepare the way we do during peacetime. Therefore, we all have to be prepared mentally and physically, to successfully complete any task that is given to us. I have also been made to understand that the enemy is a rag-tag separatist outfit, trained and equipped by our own R&AW. But we must never underestimate the enemy. We are combat soldiers and we must be prepared for any eventuality that may take place on the battlefield. My best wishes are with you and I pray to our Guru to make you victorious in your mission. Always remember, "*Deg Teg Fateh*", prosperity in peace and victory in war. God be with you. *Jo bole so nihaal*', Bubbles gave the war cry of the regiment and the Sikhs.

'*Sat sri akal!*', shouted the soldiers.

'Come Biru, walk along with me', Bubbles said.

'Tell me', he continued, 'how have you prepared for the mission?'

Sir, the number ten platoon under me will be in the first heptr and we will take over the landing zone, LZ, from 10 Para, thereby relieving them from their task. The rest of my company will land at the LZ in the subsequent heptrs. We will form a firm base and strengthen our position at the LZ. Once the battalion headquarters and Charlie company land, we will move to the task of destroying the military headquarters of the LTTE in the university. One platoon will stay put at the firm base just in case we have to fall back and also for administrative purposes later. After completion of the task, I will lead the link up with the ground forces ex 72 Inf Brigade. My success signal to you on the radio set is 'Fateh', and on-ground it will be 'ROG' (red over green). We will carry weapon scale ammunition and emergency ration sufficient for one day', he concluded.

'Good, I think you have covered all the bases. I would suggest you carry ammunition of 81mm mortar in the lead heptr. We may need it in the subsequent tasks. Why lug it all the way by ground. As a result, more troops can then go in the subsequent heptrs', Bubbles said.

'Roger Sir.'

'See you at the mounting base', Bubbles said, walking away.

Biru returned to his company and instructed Sampuran Singh to load the 81mm mortar ammunition as well. Sampuran had no idea where the ammunition was lying, especially as it was dark now. Nonetheless, along with a few soldiers, he went off in the direction of the group of men also searching for ammunition boxes.

Biru was feeling uncomfortable with the pace of preparations. Their entire stock of ammunition and equipment was strewn across the service track, and in the jet-black night, it was becoming increasingly difficult to locate them. The small arms ammunition boxes were still sealed, and the individual magazines had not been charged. This was worrying Biru. There was very little time left now. The troops had not eaten since their packed lunch at Tambaram airfield, and there was no scope for cooking at the moment. Every single man was required to lug the ammunition, stores, and equipment that was currently spread all over the tarmac. To top it all, they were also trying to find the mortar ammunition, which then had to be brought to their company location. It was already 2100 hours.

Their priority was the operation, the cooking and other administrative actions could be taken up after the link-up took place tomorrow morning, thought Biru.

'Sir, your weapon', Kartar Singh said, breaking his chain of thought.

Kartar had been Biru's buddy since he had joined the unit. He came from the farming belt of Gurdaspur in Punjab. Belonging to a poor Mazhabi Sikh family, he had seen his days of poverty. His family was very proud of him for becoming a soldier and also for being the only earning member. He took all the major family decisions despite being the youngest of four siblings.

He was taller and broader than Biru. At 6 feet and 85 kgs, he was a member of the unit's basketball and boxing team. His cheerful demeanour and his enthusiasm were infectious and he was very sought-after for all the difficult tasks. Biru and Kartar bonded well together and last summer, Biru had visited his village to attend his marriage. It was a big occasion in the village that a Major, Kartar's company commander, had come to attend his marriage. Kartar and his family were very proud of this fact.

'How many magazines?', Biru asked.

'Sir, we are still trying to locate the 9mm ammunition. I will fill them and give them to you once that is done', he replied.

'Make sure you find the ammunition before we leave', Biru said, smiling at Kartar.

'Yes Sir', Kartar saluted and walked away.

Young soldiers with no combat experience, not even trained on SHBO. What was this chaos?, Biru thought.

Biru had been posted from another battalion of the regiment to 13 Sikh LI. He had been a Commando Instructor prior to his posting to 13 Sikh LI, which was at that time in Chushul, Ladakh, at a field station. After a year, he moved with the unit to Gwalior, a peace station.

They had not yet found all the ammunition boxes. Just a few 7.62mm ammunition boxes had been located among the 81mm mortar, just enough to allow a magazine for each man. They were searching frantically. In the darkness of the night, with tons and tons of equipment, stores, tents, rations, ammunition, weapons, and men distributed all over the tarmac, with the rain having played havoc not too long ago, locating boxes of ammunition and grenades was seeming to be a herculean task.

Biru wanted to avail of some toilet facilities and could not see any around. The ATC seemed about 700 metres from his location and he did not want to risk going there when he did not know the route to it. He could not hold it in any longer, and as was universally common to combat soldiers the world over, he had to urinate before he went into an operation. A grassy dark patch next to the service track served this purpose.

After he had finished, Kartar suddenly appeared from nowhere and offered him water to wash his hands.

Biru walked into the night, away from all the chaos around him. He wanted to smoke in peace and confirm his plan. But suddenly, his mind drifted away to his wife and child. He had left them home in a rush. No long goodbyes or hugs and parting kisses. Just a 'see you soon' peck on the cheek. He was missing them already. How he longed to hold his son in his arms and feel the warmth of his wife.

'Sir, tea', Kartar said.

'You always find me Kartara', he replied with a warmth that buddies share.

'Sir, remembering home?', he asked.

'Hmmm', he replied, 'what about you?', he asked Kartar.

'Of course Sir. I have promised my wife that I will be back for her birthday in January.'

'Sure you will. But first, tell me, how did you make this tea?', Biru asked, aware that they had no means of cooking.

'Sir, we managed to get some diesel from the air force guys here', he replied with a hint of naughtiness, typical of the Sikh LI troops.

Biru did not pursue it any further. Over the years, he had learnt not to probe into such matters beyond a point. Necessity was the mother of invention, but for his troops, crisis situations were the father of innovation. He just smiled to himself. As long as they had not done anything illegal it was okay with him.

'Is everyone having tea?', he asked Kartar.

'Yes Sir'

'And you?'

'I had some', he lied.

'Kartar, you and I have been buddies for a long time now. I know you have not had the tea. So pour some for yourself from the thermos', Biru said.

Kartar did not move so Biru took the thermos from him and poured it out in the thermos mug, handing it to Kartar.

'Would you like to smoke a cigarette, Sir?', Kartar asked.

'Yes, I need one now', he replied.

Kartar took out a packet of India Kings from his pocket and gave it to Biru.

'Kartar you are a devout Sikh, correct?', he asked.

'Yes Sir', Kartar answered.

'And tobacco is strictly prohibited in Sikhism, but you still carry it for me, why?' It had always astonished Biru that Kartar was a devout Sikh and therefore never smoked, but as a buddy always carried it for Biru.

'Sir, firstly carrying is not prohibited, only smoking is.

Secondly, you are my leader, my Guru, and my saviour. You are more educated, better trained, and have a good sense of things. We all believe that you will always bring glory and victory to us. So it is my sacred duty to serve you with all that I have, this is what the Gurus have always preached', replied Kartar.

Biru was overwhelmed and was grateful that it was dark; Kartar could not see the tears of gratitude rolling down his cheeks. This was dedication and loyalty of the highest order.

'I think it is time', said Biru. It was 2330 hours when the unit started moving towards the mounting base.

It had been a hectic day for Major Sheonan Singh too—briefing, recce, and then preparing for the operation. The Para Commando company had moved into Sri Lanka along with the division. They were familiar with the terrain and the population in Jaffna, but they had never undertaken any combat operations in the area. As a matter of fact, they had had cordial relations with the locals until now.

The orders to the company were very clear, 'You may leave your rations behind, we will manage without food, but take all your ammunition, maybe a little extra as well'.

The company had recently carried out firing at the makeshift ranges in the airfield, and all of them were happy that their weapons were zeroed and grenades primed.

Sheonan walked up to a group of soldiers who were busy charging their ammunition magazines.

'How much ammunition are you boys carrying with you?', he asked.

'Sir, 20 magazines on the SLR and 400 rounds extra, and 40 magazines on each LMG, with 1000 rounds extra for it. Should we take some more?', the havildar enquired.

'I think that should suffice, although we do not know what kind of opposition we may have to face', said Sheonan.

'Sir, in most of our operations we do not know what opposition we are going to face, and in the past, whenever we have known, it was proven to be wrong the moment the first bullet was fired', replied the other.

All of them laughed in agreement.

'Good, now I know that all of you are prepared for any eventuality', Sheonan said, walking towards the next group of soldiers.

He saw Ranjit standing with his group of men and he walked up to him.

'Ranjit, do you have a clear understanding of the operation?'

'Well Sir, as clear as it can get', he replied.

'And what does that mean?'

'Sir, I think I know as much as you do', Ranjit replied.

'What is that you know? Tell me', he demanded.

'Sir, in simple terms we have been tasked to destroy the political headquarters of the LTTE in an SHBO by first light tomorrow', Ranjit told Sheonan.

'But Sir, we do not have details about the terrain, the strength and the weapons that the LTTE guys may use, what the escape routes are or the reinforcements that they can get in, whether we have any air or mortar support. There are so many questions and no answers. It's frustrating going in like this and it happens every time with us', said Nair who was standing next to Ranjit.

'Agreed Nair, that is why we have the Para Commandoes. When the situation is fluid and the details are hazy, drop the Commandoes. Who Dares Wins. That's our motto and we always live by it', Sheonan said with a sense of pride.

'Yeah, I think that is what the fun is all about', Nair replied.

Biru had reached the end of runway twenty-nine, where the mounting base was supposed to be. This was the place the heptrs would be parked, where they were supposed to mount them to go ahead with their operation. There were no heptrs. The runway had ended and there was loose soil and darkness. Biru switched on his torch and waved it all around. No heptrs. He sent three search parties to look all around. Not a trace of the heptrs.

What the f*** is this?, he thought.

'Kartar, give me the handset', he told his buddy and radio operator.

'Four for One-Five, fetch Tiger for Tiger', he said.

'Tiger One-Five listening, pass your message', came the reply from Bubbles.

'One-Five there are no birds here, I repeat, there are no birds here', said Biru.

'Roger, have you looked all around?', Bubbles asked, although knowing the answer beforehand.

'One-Five yes, nothing within 500 metres.'

'Four, Roger', said Bubbles.

'All stations One-Five, wait for further orders. Tiger Four reach me. All stations stay on listening watch', Bubbles said into the mouthpiece of the radio set.

Biru started walking back along the unit column looking for Bubbles.

Not far away, at the Jaffna university LTTE communication centre, the transmission was being monitored.

One of the NCOs of the CO protection party guided Biru to Bubbles.

'Biru, go to the ATC and ask them about the mounting base. Some f****r should know where the mounting base is. They should have informed us in case they have changed it', Bubbles was irritated now.

'Roger Sir', said Biru, and along with Kartar and another NCO, started towards the ATC where the lights in the control cabin were visible to them.

Biru estimated that the ATC would be a kilometre to the southeast of his present location. It took him a little more time as the route was longer than he had anticipated.

The duty Sergeant at the ATC called up about half a dozen people to find out the whereabouts of the mounting base and was finally told that it was further southeast from the ATC. Runway twenty-one.

Biru wanted to check it out before he moved the complete unit.

He took one of the corporals from the ATC and sent him along with the NCO to get the unit column. Then Kartar and Biru moved towards runway twenty-one.

'Four for One-Five, I have found the location of Mike Bravo (Mounting Base), moving there. I have sent Tejinder to get you. He will bring you until the Alfa, Tango, Charlie (ATC) where I will meet you over', Biru announced on the radio set.

It was pitch-dark as the moon was supposed to rise late at night. Whatever little ambient light was supposed to be present had been blocked by low clouds. A cool breeze blew across the airfield.

Biru and Kartar kept on the road that ran east from the ATC. They passed the Base Ops on their way, which seemed deserted except for a small lighted board that said 'Base Ops'.

'Halt, who goes there?', a loud command froze Biru and Kartar in their tracks.

'Sentry it is us from 13 Sikh LI', said Biru, quickly regaining his composure.

The sentry switched on his torch and approached them from behind a boundary wall.

'Jai Hind Sir', he said recognising Biru's rank epaulettes, 'Where are you going?'

'To the mounting base on runway twenty-one', he replied.

'That's quite a distance Sir, go straight on this road', he said pointing ahead of him on the road they were standing on, 'it cuts across runway twenty-two. Go about a kilometre ahead, the next runway is runway twenty-one'.

'Thank you.'

'Kartar, has the unit started?', Biru asked.

'No Sir, not yet', he answered.

It was already 0100 hours and the h-hour was 0130 hours. Biru knew they would be late to the mounting base. He hurried.

Biru and Kartar crossed runway twenty-two and after a while could see the traffic control lights of runway twenty-one.

The taillights of the heptrs were visible, and as he moved closer, he saw the soldiers of 10 Para getting into the heptrs. It was already 0120 hours, ten minutes remained to h-hour.

On seeing Biru, the flight commander Winco Sapre called out to him from the heptr.

'Good morning, have you guys finally reached?', he asked Biru.

'Well Sir, it will take a while for the unit to reach, I am sorry we did not know the location of the mounting base, and it took us a while to get here', he replied.

'Sure, we will have to wait, we have no choice', replied the Winco.

He sounded annoyed because of the delay.

'Where have you been Biru?', Sheonan said as he stepped out of the shadows of the heptr.

'Well Sir, long story short, we got lost', Biru replied.

'Yeah, I know this is a hastily put together f****** operation. You be careful Biru. I realise that there will be a delay of at least an hour now. Well, can't do much but wait', Sheonan said.

'I hope you all are carrying enough ammunition', asked a concerned Sheonan.

'Yes Sir, as a matter of fact, the CO has also told me to carry the 81mm mortar ammunition so that the later heptrs can carry more men', he said.

'Are you guys out of minds?', Sheonan raised his voice, 'What are you going to do with that ammunition?'

'Sir, COs orders are orders and we may need them at a later stage', he replied rather innocently.

'Well, these are your plans, I cannot say much', Sheonan responded.

The four MI8s were sitting on the tarmac, with the pilots carrying out the pre-take off checks. The pilots and the co-pilots were locked inside the cockpits, directing the Commandoes who were now mounting the heptr.

The unit arrived much before they had anticipated. They made double quick time by jogging all the way. It was around 0200 hours by the time the tail of the unit column moved into the mounting base.

'ATC Karan formation, ready for take-off', said Sapre into the mouthpiece of his wireless set.

Sapre was the task force commander and captain of the leading heptr, along with Flight Lieutenant Vinayraj as his co-pilot.

The first wave consisted of all the four heptrs divided into two wicks each. The second wick was led by Squardon Leader Doraiswami and Flying Officer Prakash, and was scheduled to take off after a time gap of seven minutes. This was the flying time to the LZ, and they did not want the second wick of heptrs to become vulnerable to ground fire as they waited for the first wick to clear the LZ.

Two heptrs of the first wick that carried the pathfinders, took off at 0200 hours, thirty minutes after h-hour.

Bubbles was not too concerned about the h-hour as there were no other troops to really coordinate the h-hour with.

Ranjit was in the leading heptr, followed by Sheonan in the second.

The heptrs took off facing east, heading towards Jaffna university.

Biru had assembled his company and they had formed up in the sequence that they were to mount the heptrs.

The operation had already been delayed by thirty minutes.

The cool breeze was still blowing across the airfield and the cloud cover had moved lower on the route to the university.

The second wick also took off after two minutes, maintaining a timed distance between the first wick.

The cloud cover moved still lower but did not pose any threat to the pilots as they were flying just about 100 feet above the ground. The route in and out for the heptrs was clear of any obstacles that could have hindered them.

Between Sapre and Vinayraj, they had about 2,000

hours of flying experience, and the flight from Palaly airfield to the university was not one that would challenge their flying skills. The weather was conducive for flying, and in spite of the dark night, the ambient lights emanating from the area around the university were enough to guide them to the open area that they had seen during their daylight recce. A tall building to the west was well lit and served as an additional navigational aid to them.

In the silence of the night, the *thud thud* of the heptrs main rotors sounded like hundreds of elephants stomping their feet together.

The hatch of the MI8 was already open and two slithering ropes were tied to the bar on top. The pathfinders, led by Ranjit, were ready for the captain's command to start the slithering. Sapre was guiding his heptr towards the open area, which he could now clearly see as he flew the bird in.

'Approaching Delta Zebra in one-zero seconds', his voice crackled on the speaker next to the slithering bar.

Two commandoes got ready to drop the sandbags tied to the end of the slithering ropes. The heptr started to descend. Vinayraj was keeping an eye on the altimeter and calling out the altitude.

'Seventy, fifty, forty, thirty…steadying', Vinayraj said.

Sapre steadied the heptr at 30 feet.

Hovering a heptr is the most difficult of all the

manoeuvres. On a dark night with low visibility, it becomes extremely difficult for the pilot to know the relative height of the aircraft. Any miscalculation can become disastrous.

Being an experienced pilot, Sapre ceased the forward directional flying of the heptr, easing back on the cyclic until its forward motion stopped and the aircraft remained motionless over a point on the ground.

The cricket pitch on the ground served well as a fixed point that he could use to detect small changes in the aircraft's altitude or attitude.

Finally, he adjusted the collective to maintain a fixed altitude, and the foot pedals to steady the direction in which the helicopter was pointing.

He had to maintain a stabilized hover for the commandoes to safely slither down. Any jerk or movement could put the lives of these slithering commandoes in danger.

The light on the port side of the hatch turned red to green, and the two commandoes threw out the sandbags with the slithering ropes tied to them. The heptr was steady and as the bags landed on the ground below, the rope became taut.

Ranjit and his buddy commenced the slithering.

Halfway down the rope, Ranjit's left foot got entangled in the cord, and before he could realise it, his hand grip came off the rope and he was dangling upside down.

The next commando on the rope was ready to go but had to stop when he saw that Ranjit had still not cleared the rope.

Ranjit's buddy on the second rope adjusted the sandbag and was ready to receive the next commando on his rope. He looked around for Ranjit and could not see him next to the first rope's sandbag. He then realised that Ranjit was dangling upside down. He left his post and moved to free Ranjit by picking up the sandbag so his rope would slacken a bit, and Ranjit could hold it to pull himself up.

Sapre, looking out of the cockpit window, was getting restless as he thought the slithering had still not commenced.

Ranjit got hold of the slacked part of the rope and pulled himself up. Then, with his right hand, he managed to untangle his foot and slithered down. He patted his buddy on the shoulder, expressing both his gratitude and a signal for him to go back to his rope.

The rest of the pathfinder team slithered without any delay.

The second heptr also came in as planned, and Sheonan and his team slithered down and took up positions all around the open area, which they had by now realised was a football field surrounded by an athletics track.

The pathfinders were on the ground.

The second wick was being commanded by Sqn Ldr Doriaswamy, with Prakash and Sonpar in the next heptr. Doraiswamy landed and the commandoes in his heptr dismounted without much ado.

Prakash had seen the drop zone, or DZ, during the day recce, albeit from a distance. As he approached the DZ, he realised his mistake. This did not seem like the DZ he had seen during the day. It was too near the village and far from the university. The area was surrounded by tall coconut trees, and landing could be dangerous.

He and Sonpar unanimously decided that it would be prudent to turn back and fly in again with the next wick. They would not drop the Para Commandoes in a DZ they were not sure about.

Biru realised that there was some confusion when the second heptr landed and flew off again without taking in a fresh load of the commandoes.

Prakash had already spoken to Sapre while approaching the airfield, and he had been cleared to land. He would now follow Sapre to the correct DZ. When he was at the DZ, he realised that the earlier one was about 800 metres to his east and it would have been disastrous for the Commandoes to have been dropped there. He looked towards Sonpar, who gave him a thumbs up for making the right decision of returning to Palaly airfield and coming in again with Sapre.

Prakash had never been shot at before, and maybe that is why he did not realise it when the LMG bullet hit his pilot seat's headrest. It had missed his head by millimetres. Coming in through the windshield, it had made a clean hole in it and the seat. Before he could look back to assess the damage, all hell broke loose from the top of the university building.

'Go, go, go', shouted Sapre into the mouthpiece of his headset.

The bullets were raining on them, now hitting the heptrs with more accuracy. Prakash put the heptr on full throttle and turned it eastwards, getting out of the rooftop's effective fire reach. The heptr was still in the range of the LMGs and was severely hit at several places.

The commando teams on the ground had also been pinned down. The LTTE fighters had an advantage from their position on higher ground, coupled with the intimate knowledge of the area. The lack of cover available to the commandoes made them sitting ducks. Some LTTE fighters were also firing from the lanes adjacent to the university building. They came out into the open from the lanes, fired, and disappeared. These young boys were in *lungis* and vests and seemed just like other Tamilian boys.

Ranjit had moved with his team to the west of the DZ and was firing into the lanes from where the LTTE fighters were making their appearance. The other LTTE fighters in the university building could not be seen, as they were either on the rooftops or inside the building firing from the windows. The flashes coming out of the flash hider could be seen from nearly all the windows.

Seven heptr loads of a total of 140 commandoes had landed at the Jaffna University DZ. They moved into four teams of thirty-five each—Alpha Team led by Ranjit, Bravo team by Sheonan, Charlie team by Nair, and Delta team by Capt Vellore, who was also their doctor. All the teams fanned out in the cardinal directions making use of whatever cover they could find in the area.

Ranjit readjusted the position of his team to provide suppressing fire to Sheonan's and Nair's team so that some of the pressure could be lifted from them, and they could then move to more tactically advantageous positions. The LTTE fighters were unforgiving, and relentlessly kept up the heavy volume of fire on the teams. Crawling on their bellies and moving under near accurate fire, the teams moved behind the few trees that they could find.

Sapre and Prakash landed at the Palaly airfield for the next lift. Sapre gestured to Biru to get into the heptrs with his team. Sapre spoke to the other pilots and warned them of the heavy fire that they were drawing from the university building.

'We will keep going in and dropping these guys off as long as these machines are fit for flying, so be ready to take fire boys. Best of luck', he said before they took off for the next sortie.

Biru could now hear the firing from the university area and his team looked anxiously at him. With hardly any time to prepare for the mission, the team members had just one SLR magazine charged and loaded on their weapons. The rest of their ammunition was still in the ammunition boxes stored with the belief that they would have enough time to charge the balance of the magazines at the DZ. This error in planning would cost them heavily during the impending operation.

Sheonan was leading his team towards one of the alleys from where they were being fired at. The LTTE fighters came out of these alleys repeatedly, to fire rockets and AK-47s at them. They were returning fire but it was not as effective as they wanted it to be.

As the two heptrs flew in towards the DZ, they started drawing heavy fire from the rooftops again. They were hit many times and damaged badly. It was a miracle that none of the vitals of the heptrs was harmed. Undeterred, the pilots kept flying their machines into the DZ.

Mahattaya and Yogi were personally directing the fire from the rooftop. When the first two heptrs came in, they instructed their fighters to hold their fire and let the pathfinders slither down and take up positions. They were deciphering the direction of the fly-in and fly-out routes to the DZ and also wanted the complete teams to come in. They then re-positioned and re-sited their automatic weapons to ensure that they covered the entire DZ for the subsequent drops. They had planned to destroy, or at least make the heptrs unflyable at the DZ, so that they could be displayed as war trophies and become a cause of immense embarrassment to the IPKF. Now they were ready, having covered the entire area with automatics, rockets, and small arms fire.

The two heptrs with Biru's team of one officer, one JCO, and twenty-seven soldiers, landed in the DZ as planned, amidst heavy firing between the Para commandoes and the LTTE fighters. The Commandoes were trying to keep the LTTE fighters' heads down so that Biru's team could land safely. But perched on higher ground, and with their snipers picking their target with impunity, it was a no-win situation for them. Nonetheless, the heavy volume of fire at full capacity did keep the LTTE's heads down for a while, until Biru and his team alighted from the heptr.

Bullets from the automatics pierced the MI8's aluminium body, luckily missing the crew who had no idea where the fire was coming from. Only the flashes were visible to them. Biru's team dismounted amidst heavy firing. Totally disoriented in the darkness that engulfed the DZ, the area around the platoon was in disarray. Biru tried his best to be heard over the cacophony of the heptr rotor and the gunfire. The soldiers who had dismounted did not know what to do. The lack of training, fatigue, disorientation, and enemy firing overwhelmed everyone, the young and the experienced soldiers alike.

Biru was now holding onto each one of them consecutively and yelling instructions into their ears. A few of them started recovering and followed the instruction being given to them. Sub Sampuran Singh was also pushing and shoving a few soldiers to take up positions around the heptr.

The heptr sergeant realised that they had not yet unloaded their ammunition. He shouted at the nearest soldier lying near the hatch.

'Unload your ammunition quickly, we are under fire and the heptr may not be able to take off in case the engine is hit', he shouted.

Four soldiers started unloading the boxes, which also included the mortar ammunition.

As the last box was unloaded, a burst of bullets hit one of the soldiers who dropped dead.

'Clear for take-off', shouted the sergeant into the mouthpiece of his headphone.

Sapre put the heptr in full throttle and took off. By

now, he knew that his heptr had been hit several times and some vital parts had been damaged.

There was smoke billowing from Sapre's aircraft as he steadied it on course to Palaly.

'I think the fuel pipeline has been hit, the fuel gauge is showing the fuel declining too fast', he told his co-pilot.

'We have enough fuel to make it back', his co-pilot replied.

The seven minutes journey back to the airfield seemed like seven hours but Sapre finally landed his heptr safely. The fire tenders were already lined up to douse the fire, which they did rather rapidly.

Sapre was happy to see Prakash following and landing after him. Throughout the flight from the DZ to the airfield, Prakash had followed Sapre's heptr so in case he made an emergency landing, Prakash could evacuate him and the co-pilot.

It was obvious that these heptrs could not be flown again in the near future. The flight engineer's team was busy assessing the damage to the aircraft.

As he landed back at the airfield his fears were confirmed by the flight engineer. Three heptrs were declared unfit to fly.

With a heavy heart, Sapre broke the news to the Col GS, who was now on the tarmac.

The GOC was informed about the predicament, and

he immediately took a decision to abort the mission, which was otherwise a foregone conclusion. With the heptrs unable to fly, there was no way the rest of the unit of 13 Sikh LI could be air inserted at Jaffna university.

Bubbles was heartbroken and furious. He walked up to the GOC who was taking a first-hand account of the situation. The heptrs were visibly heavily damaged, and even a non-technical man like him could also assess that it would be impossible to fly the machines. Sapre's heptr had two punctures in the fuel tank and the pedal wiring had been severed, the next one had its collective wiring completely damaged, and the third heptr's main controls had been hit, shattering the system. It was a tribute to the expertise of all the pilots that they had managed to get the heptrs back to Palaly airfield.

'Sir, there will be a massacre at the university if the rest of the unit is not flown in immediately there. Your decision to abort the mission at this moment is not correct', a desperate and agitated Bubbles said.

'I understand where you are coming from Bubbles, but there is no way we can fly these machines anymore. Sadly, we do not even have the spares to repair them. According to Groupy (Group Captain) MP Premi, all of them will require base repairs, and a team coming in from Tambaram with the required spares to make them serviceable. That definitely cannot happen in the time frame that we would want it to happen', Harkirat replied.

'But Sir, we cannot leave the teams there on their own. I suggest that I be allowed to move by road. I can link up with HQ 72 Inf brigade and 4/5 GR', Bubbles proposed, urgency in his voice.

'I think that is a good idea, go ahead. Hoshiyar, muster up all the transport that is available here, and allot it to Bubbles', he replied, instructing his Col GS.

'Roger Sir', the Col GS confirmed.

Fresh orders were passed by Harkirat.

'Bubbles, your unit 13 Sikh LI minus one platoon, will now advance along the Palaly-Vasivilan-Urumpirai axis. You will establish contact with 4/5 GR, which is also on the same axis. Once contact had been established with 4/5 GR, further orders will follow', Harkirat said.

'Sir, when you say battalion, I hope you realise that we are 13 Sikh LI minus two companies and a platoon—A and B company, which has not been transported yet, and a platoon of Delta company, which has already been dropped at the university', Bubbles said.

THE LINK UP

CHAPTER 8

THAT NEVER HAPPENED

A sense of urgency took over the unit, and Bubbles immediately passed the executive orders to his adjutant, to move the unit to the main entrance of the airfield.

At 0300 hours the rest of the unit started moving on the road, towards Jaffna University.

The unit got onto the road axis that they had to follow. With no maps and no knowledge of the road system here, Bubbles presumed that they were on the correct path, the one Col GS had indicated to them.

13 Sikh LI was at a gap of about 2 kilometres from 4/5 GR, which was leading the advance.

At around 0400 hours, when they had moved only a

few kilometres, a concealed IED blew up on the road, under the wheels of the leading 3-ton truck. Simultaneously, automatic small arms fire opened up from all directions onto them. Again, the leading platoon of soldiers reacted in the same way as Biru's platoon had. No reactions. They all froze, not knowing how to react for a few seconds until the first two soldiers were hit by LTTE fire.

Not prepared for this kind of reception, there was surprise and numbness that manifested into a lack of reaction from many of the younger soldiers. But in a few minutes, their training instincts took over, and every single one of them fell into the battle drill of dash, down, crawl, observe, and fire.

All the soldiers immediately took up positions astride the road and started returning fire.

The IED was made up of 15 kgs of plastic explosives, embedded with nails, ball bearings, and other pieces of iron. In all, five soldiers had died with their body parts strewn all over the roadside, and six were in various injured conditions.

The remaining members of the unit reached the roadside and took up positions. The ones closer to the explosion were still in shock. It had hardly been six hours since they had landed at Palaly, and the unit had already faced their dead and wounded.

Bubbles shouted for the regimental medical officer (RMO), with his team of battlefield nursing assistants (BFNAs), to move ahead.

He quickly collected himself and stood up, dusting off the mud and debris from the explosion. A few of the soldiers who were close to the explosion site mainly suffered concussions and minor injuries due to the flying debris. They were attended to by the medical team.

The unit has been baptised by fire.

Bubbles' operator was still trying to establish contact with Biru's team. He was getting restless and his instincts told him that all was not well with the team.

Bravo company was pinned down as the LTTE fighters were in concealed positions and were bringing down effective fire on them. Bubbles immediately got on to the radio set and asked Chhangani, the Bravo company commander, about the situation ahead of him.

'One-Five for Two, Sitrep (Situation Report)?', he asked.

'Two for One-Five, we are under effective fire but have taken up positions. Two confirmed fatal. A few injuries. Will try to move them back. Presently pinned down', Chhangani said.

'Will you be able to clear the enemy position?', Bubbles asked.

'Negative, I repeat negative.'

'Roger. Has the enemy been sighted?'

'Yes, and I have been able to fix him', replied Chhangani meaning that the LTTE fighters were unable able to move out of their positions without suffering casualties.

'Good work', said Bubbles. 'One-Five for Three-Tiger, message, over', he continued.

'Three-Tiger for One Five, pass your message, over', replied Major Srichand, who was the company commander.

'Are you under fire?', asked Bubbles.

'Negative', Srichand replied.

'Move ahead and clear the opposition. I say again, move ahead and clear the opposition.'

'Move ahead and clear opposition, Roger that, Tiger One-Five', repeated Srichand, to confirm the executive orders.

'Best of luck and stay in touch, out to you', said Bubbles.

'One-Five to One-Tiger, message, over', Bubbles continued.

Major Rakesh Mohan, who was on listening watch, immediately came on air.

'One-Tiger for One-Five, pass your message, over', responded Rakesh.

'Move ahead and establish a fire base and provide covering fire in case required. Also, be ready to reinforce, for which orders will follow', said Bubbles.

'One-five for Three, provide firm base to Two', he instructed.

Rakesh confirmed the executive orders and started moving his company ahead, coordinating with Srichand to establish the location of the firm and fire base.

This was a classic quick attack, in so far as the timings were concerned. With the companies moving close to each other, the time to move into positions and establish the firm and fire base would be very little. This the unit had practised several times, and it did not take elaborate orders to execute the plan.

Bravo company had taken up positions astride the road leading to the crossing of the roads Vallai-Tellippalai-Araly and Palaly-Urumpirai. They were drawing fire from the heavily wooded area, about 300 metres to their east. The LTTE fighters had taken up well-fortified and concealed positions in the woods, and the few huts in the area. A few snipers were also in positions on coconut trees and curbed all movements by the soldiers.

With his leading platoon almost pinned down, Chhangani could only make minor readjustments to fix the LTTE positions and make sure they did not carry out any readjustments when Srichand or Mohan went in for their task. He had secured the area and made sure that the LTTE fighters could not physically interfere with the preparations for the attack.

His BFNAs had crawled up ahead and were desperately trying to move the dead and wounded. Capt Trivedi, the RMO, had by now established a make-shift regimental aid post (RAP) to receive and treat them.

Srichand's company also started drawing fire as they neared the area of contact. With no knowledge of the terrain, and the unilluminated night sky, there was the lurking danger of sections and platoon getting disoriented and going off in the wrong direction. Therefore, their movement was deliberate and slow, with each man staying within visual distance, which in this darkness, meant about 2 feet. The rain, which had held up until now, suddenly started pouring down on them torrentially. A dark night of heavy rain, fatigue, hunger, and disorientation, with the enemy firing at you like there was no tomorrow, all within six hours of landing on foreign soil for the first time, was the worst situation one could be in.

Srichand's Charlie company was now alongside Bravo and started taking up positions in the firm base. He arranged his platoon in the order of attack and waited for Mohan to give him the green signal that the fire base had been established, so that the attack team could move in.

As Mohan moved ahead with his leading platoon to

establish the fire base, the LTTE fighters opened fire with all they had, moving out of their positions. The fighters rushed the leading elements of Mohan's Alpha company who were in the dark and did not realise their presence until the enemy was at bayoneting distance, within 2-3 feet.

Srichand realised that Mohan may not be able to give him the covering fire he so desperately required for the attack to begin. He moved in with his leading platoon to support Mohan. With just a few casualties, the LTTE fighters retreated into the coconut plantation, carrying their wounded with them.

Mohan quickly established the fire base and started shooting to cover Charlie's movement.

Charlie's leading platoon, with Srichand at the forefront, started moving towards the LTTE's position. It had hardly been a minute when all the fire from the LTTE positions stopped. Not a bullet.

'STOP FIRE!', Srichand shouted.

There was pin drop silence.

The LTTE fighters were no longer firing at them. Silence.

By now, the leading platoon had reached the edge of the coconut plantation and was tactically moving in towards the huts.

There was no movement and not a single shot was fired.

Srichand fired from his carbine trying to draw retaliatory shots from the LTTE.

Nothing.

They went from hut to hut and searched the complete area. Not a soul. A few drops of blood, but that was all.

It suddenly struck Srichand that the LTTE fighters had inflicted casualties on them and delayed them by at least an hour. That was their aim and they had achieved it.

'Three for One-Five, all clear', said Srichand into the mouthpiece of the radio set.

'Mohan', said Bubbles as he moved ahead to catch up with him and take a first-hand account of the operation, 'they have delayed us by an hour. The fact that they did not give us a pitched battle means that they have their main defences somewhere up ahead. Our move by road caught them by surprise, and to gain time to consolidate their main defences, they set up this delaying position', he said.

'I think your assessment is absolutely correct, Sir. Otherwise, being in an advantageous position, they should have given us a pitched battle. We have to be very careful as we move ahead', Mohan replied.

'Yes, better be. But you must remember Mohan, we are fighting against time. Biru is stuck with the Para Commandoes at the university, and we have to reach him at the earliest. So move fast, but be careful. Follow section leading and platoon tactics. Get back to basics. One foot on the ground, move cover-to-cover, fire and move again', Bubbles said.

'I understand that it is a great shock for all of us to have lost some of our Sheras or have them seriously wounded. But this should not be a setback for us, as a matter of fact, it should strengthen our resolve to complete our mission. Now that we are aware that the whole route to Jaffna may be strewn with IEDs and there might be ambushes ahead, we have to tread carefully. Make sure that the basic infantry drills of section leading platoon tactics are followed, and move with one foot on the ground', he told his company commanders and the rest of the group as they huddled beside him, behind a hut.

'Mohan', he said to the second-in-command, 'Bring Charlie's strength up from the other groups. Alpha company will lead now, followed by Bravo, HQ, and then Charlie. Be ready to move in fifteen minutes. All of you have to lead from the front, do not let the men think that our morale is low. All the best, now get going', concluded Bubbles.

The 2IC went about redistributing the strength of the companies, trying to make up an ad hoc platoon.

'Let's get going', Bubbles said.

THE LONELY BATTLE

CHAPTER 9

I HAVE NO ORDERS TO MOVE OUT

'One-Five for Tiger-Four, One-Five for Tiger-Four', Bubbles' operator was desperately trying to establish contact with Biru, unaware of the fact that his radio set had been destroyed. Bubbles wanted Biru to know that the heli-landing had been aborted, and the rest of the unit was now moving by road to meet up with them.

Biru and his team had moved just a few metres after unloading the ammunition from the heptrs and were pinned down by the LTTE fire coming onto them. They were on the ground without any cover except for the darkness, which was like a double-edged weapon. Although they had taken up positions all around, it was futile as they could not see the LTTE fighters.

The lame heptrs had flown back, and the teams of Sikh LI and the Para Commandoes were now in enemy territory, totally exposed with no help coming whatsoever.

It was completely dark except for the flashes of small arms firing, and intermittently, the RPG rocket's impact could be seen on the DZ.

The Para commando teams had fanned out to the periphery of the ground and were engaging the LTTE fighters, who were now trying to close in and overwhelm their positions.

'Kartar, get me Tiger One-Five', said Biru, presuming that Kartar was next to him as he was his buddy and his radio operator as well.

There was no reply.

'Kartar, did you hear me? Get me Tiger One-Five', shouted Biru, trying to be heard over the sound of the fire coming in, and various commanders shouting combat commands.

There was still no reply.

Biru turned around to look for Kartar in the direction he thought the latter should have been.

The cloud cover had moved and there was some ambient light on the ground.

Biru saw Kartar lying about 6 feet away from him with the radio set case still strapped on his back, completely shattered by a burst of bullets. There was blood splattered on the ground, still oozing from Kartar's body.

Biru crawled towards him and turned him on his side. He realised that the bullets that had hit the radio set had pierced through it and then entered Kartar's body from his shoulders, blowing his chest apart. He must have died instantly.

The radio set was completely destroyed and in no condition to work.

Biru was now no longer in communication with his battalion headquarters.

He got hold of the nearest soldier and send him looking for Subedar Sampuran Singh, who was the platoon commander. The bullets flying at them were getting deadlier and more accurate by the second, and the entire team was pinned to their places. Even a minor move invited a volley of fire.

Sampuran crawled up to Biru and informed him that his section had moved about 50 metres to the east and had taken up positions.

'You try and establish contact with the Commandoes who may be ahead of you. We have to relieve them so that they can move out for their task', he instructed Sampuran.

'Roger Sir', Sampuran replied.

He immediately moved back to his section and

started inching towards the anticipated location of the commandoes. The two leading scouts were moving very cautiously under intense fire from the LTTE fighters.

Ranjit's team was the first one to establish contact with these scouts. In their rush to launch the operation, the teams had forgotten to exchange any codewords for identification, but Gurinder, the leading scout, was a clever soldier and he spoke to the first Para commando he met in Punjabi. He immediately understood and acknowledged the commando as a Sikh LI soldier.

Sampuran moved up to Ranjit and informed him that he and his team had come to relieve them of this area.

Ranjit did not want to stay here any longer and was grateful to see Sampuran.

'The LTTE fighters are in large numbers, I do not know how many but there may be at least 100 to 150 of them. They are spread across the lanes in front', Ranjit said, indicating the clump of houses and the lanes in between them.

'Then you also have them on the rooftops and maybe in the coconut plantation to your right; the fire seems to be coming from all over. I suggest you dig in because that is the only way you can hold on to this area, otherwise they will overrun you', Ranjit advised.

'Yes Sir', Sampuran replied.

Ranjit passed on orders to his team to disengage and start moving to the east of the field, under the cover of the nearby houses, from where there was no shooting so far. He appreciated the possibility that the LTTE fighters had not spread until that area.

Sampuran moved from soldier to soldier, passing instructions to them to dig in slit trenches so they could get some cover and defensibility. It was then that they realised they were not carrying any digging tools, and the next best thing they had were their bayonets and mess tins. The dry rations kept in the mess tins for the next day were taken out to make them useful, and the soldiers started to dig.

Although the ground was soggy with the torrential rains, the mess tins were no match for its stubbornness. This, coupled with the heavy volume of fire and the fear of the LTTE fighters rushing onto their positions, made the digging very slow and laborious. But they were digging for their lives. Sampuran kept moving from soldier to soldier, motivating them to dig, fire, dig.

It often takes a person a few seconds to realise that he has been hit by a bullet, especially when it does not kill him instantly. The shock precedes the pain, and then the feeling of molten iron burning inside his vitals makes him scream in pain.

Sampuran was hit by a volley of four bullets from

an LMG. The first bullet got him on the left side of his abdomen and then the rest went in the 10 o'clock direction till his right shoulder, with two ripping his intestines. He was thrown off his feet and now lay on his back, bleeding profusely. His buddy desperately tried to stop the flow of the blood with the first field dressing (FFD) that he was carrying but to no avail.

'Do not worry about me Shera, keep the LTTE guys away from this area. The rest of the unit has to land and we have to secure this location. Go, go ahead and be with your team. There is nothing you can do for me', Sampuran said.

***

Biru was moving ahead with his team, trying to establish contact with Sheonan and his unit. They were somewhere west of the DZ and had to be relieved. It was getting late and Biru did not want their mission to be jeopardised because he was too late to relieve them.

The leading scout of his team did not stand a chance when he came under heavy LMG fire from the rooftop. He died instantaneously, his body riddled with countless bullets. The second scout took two to his upper thigh and lower torso. He fell over. Biru moved to him and took out his and the scout's FFD from their side pack, administering whatever first aid he could. The scout was crying in pain, which understandably could not be heard in the cacophony of the automatics firing.

Sheonan was waiting impatiently for Biru and his team, as the other two teams under Ranjit and Nair had already reached the rendezvous point, the RV. Any further delays could reveal their location to the LTTE fighters, which would mean more trouble, additional setbacks, and the loss of the surprise element of their impending mission.

Sheonan's radio set was functional, and he was aware that the heliborne ops had been called off. No more 13 Sikh LI troops would be landing here.

'Biru, the rest of your unit is not coming. The heptrs have been badly damaged and the GOC has aborted the mission. Your unit is now moving by road to Jaffna. I suggest you move along with us and get out of this shit hole', Sheonan said.

'But Sir, I have received no such information and I have my CO's orders to hold the DZ until the unit has safely landed here', he replied.

'Try and understand Biru, if they were going to come they would have come in by now. The fact that not even one heptr has returned in the last twenty minutes is indication enough that it has been called off. I have been told by my 2IC that the mission is off. Believe me', Sheonan pleaded.

'Sir, orders are orders. What if the unit lands after I abandon the DZ? They will be massacred. I will be scarred for life, left to feel like a coward who abandoned his post in the face of the enemy. What will I tell my boys and my people when I go back to my village? It is better to die as a Rajput than to live as a coward', Biru reasoned.

'Biru, remember when you were my student, and I saved you once, during the commando training?', he asked.

'Yes Sir', replied Biru.

'I may not be able to save you today, Biru. Please listen to me', he tried to convince him again.

'Sir, you will be late for your mission. I suggest you move out quickly with your team.'

Sheonan knew that it was futile trying to convince Biru to move out from the DZ with his team.

'Best of luck Biru, see you', Sheonan said, knowing full well that getting out of here alive would require a miracle.

Sheonan moved out swiftly with his team and headed to the RV, where he found the waiting teams now engaged in a firefight with the LTTE. His fears had come true. The delay and the thinning out of the teams from the DZ had indicated to the LTTE fighters that some of the soldiers were moving out, and they closed in on the RV immediately.

Sheonan found the area surrounded on three sides, his teams fighting to keep them at bay. He announced his arrival to Ranjit on the walkie and instructed them to break contact and move eastwards, where he would meet them by circumventing the LTTE positions.

All the teams got together, and Sheonan counted the casualties. They had five dead already.

'The dead and the wounded will be carried', he instructed his team.

'Let's move ahead and start looking for the HQ of the LTTE. Instruct the leading scouts to look out for a local and try to get some information about the HQ from him. Maybe he knows about it or has seen some high-ranking LTTE fighters here or maybe even seen a large number of them regularly at one place. That will be an indication of their HQ', Sheonan said.

Ranjit and Nair volunteered to move with the head of the column and get some information about the LTTE.

They moved out of their RV and started following a narrow road that turned away from the village. They crossed the Palaly-Jaffna railway line that cut across the road. The lane was lined with coconut trees on both sides, with a few houses along the lane. With no idea where they were or where they were going, Sheonan told Nair to find out their location from a local.

Ranjit saw an old man standing outside one of these houses, looking at the marching soldiers with curiosity. He pointed him out to Nair.

'He is our man', Ranjit said.

Nair indicated to the column to stop and take up positions on both sides of the road.

He then walked up to the old man and gestured to him to come closer, which he did without any hesitation. Nair was a Tamilian and therefore fluent in the language. He spoke to the old man for a while, asking him about the whereabouts of the LTTE HQ or any place where he had seen a large gathering of the LTTE cadres. The old man seemed to acknowledge the question asked and nodded his head, agreeing that he knew of such a place.

Sheonan instructed Nair to tell the old man to lead the way for them and take them to the place where the LTTE HQ was located.

The old man started walking and gestured for them to follow. The teams, who were waiting in a crouched position along the road stood up, and with Ranjit and Nair leading again, they started following the old man. After about 50 metres he took a turn off the road, onto a foot trail inside the coconut plantation.

Sheonan noted that there had been three huts where they had found the old man. Just an observation that he kept at the back of his head.

Ranjit was about 2 or 3 metres behind the old man,

maintaining visual contact but also keeping a reactionary distance from him. Suddenly, the old man looked back and ran off into the plantation. Before Ranjit or Nair could react, all hell broke loose. There was small arms fire from all directions and Ranjit shouted, 'Ambush, Ambush!'

Sheonan shouted instructions to the soldiers, 'To the huts behind us, move, move!'

The LTTE fighters were moving out of their positions and firing at the leading team. The leading scouts and another commando were hit fatally and fell. Nair and Ranjit kept firing from their weapons at their hips and moved ahead to evacuate them. The team behind covered their move. With another buddy pair moving ahead, they started dragging their fallen comrades behind. Sheonan and the remnants of the two teams also moved to extricate the team ahead of them.

The teams quickly disengaged and withdrew from the area, and with one team covering the move of another, they started moving towards the three huts.

Ranjit's team kept the LTTE fighters at bay and did not let them move ahead or interfere with the movement of the other teams.

Sheonan's team entered one of the huts and told the residents to move out. The team took up defensive positions inside the hut.

Similarly, Ranjit's and Nair's teams moved into the other two huts, told the residents to move out, and took up positions inside. They could see the LTTE fighters taking up positions around the huts, trying to move closer.

These huts were well constructed with a roof of fire tiles. They had a big living room with three windows facing the road and two others on either side. Behind this were two bedrooms and a kitchen, with a door at a rear exit. Each hut had a four feet high peripheral compound wall with a gate that opened onto the road.

***

Naik Amrik Singh of Biru's team was on the LMG with his number two, Sepoy Balbir Singh. They were on the eastern flank of the DZ when suddenly, four LTTE fighters came charging at them firing from their AKs, emerging from the bushes that had not been visible to Amrik until now. They were still about 10-15 feet from them when Amrik swiftly and quickly turned his LMG in their direction and fired from his hip, letting the automatic fire, controlling the trigger to let out bursts of three or four rounds. Sepoy Balbir took bullets all over his body and fell immediately. Amrik kept his position steady, holding the LMG more firmly and firing on the automatic mode downing the

LTTE fighters one after another. The leading one was hit under the belly and his momentum broke, causing him to fall a few feet from him. The last fighter managed to reach him as the magazine of the LMG had emptied out. Luckily for him, the LTTE fighter's magazine was also empty, and on realising this, he pounced on Amrik.

Amrik was a tall, burly man and resisted the impact of the LTTE fighter, who was physically no match for him.

The LTTE fighter had the bayonet of the AK-47 in his hand. Even in the darkness, Amrik could see the glint of the weapon.

He swiftly moved his right hand, and from the sheath he unleashed his most deadly and faithful weapon, the Kirpan.

The Kirpan was a silver-coloured stainless steel blade that curved at a 60 degree angle near the tip. On it was engraved,

> '*Dehi Shiva bar mohe the subh karman se kabhi na taron, na daron ari son jab jai laron, nichey kar apni jeet karon.*
>
> (O' God give me these boons, never shall I fear when I go to fight the enemy and with surety I shall attain victory).'

Both of them were now like predators ready to pounce

on each other with their weapons. Amrik held the Kirpan in the traditional way, with the blade facing upwards, while the LTTE fighter held the bayonet parallel to the ground.

The LTTE fighter attacked first, stabbing in the air violently as he moved toward Amrik, who moved very fast for a man of his size. The blade of Amrik's Kirpan just melted into the waist of the fighter, ripping open a gash about 5 inches above his hip bone. He screamed in pain but the sound was drowned out by the firing. He came back with the swiftness and violence of an injured animal. Amrik tried to step back but the bayonet went into his left shoulder. He felt the cold iron blade cut between his collar bone and the ball and socket joint. He screamed in pain as his arm went limp.

Amrik attacked almost simultaneously and the blade of the Kirpan entered the belly of the fighter. He fell backwards onto the ground but got up fast before Amrik could take advantage of the situation. Both of them were bleeding, the fighter from the belly, desperately trying to keep his internal organs inside, and Amrik from his shoulder.

Amrik spread his legs to steady his stance. The LTTE fighter pounced on him again as if making a final bid to kill him. With his left hand, he blocked Amrik's right which was holding the Kirpan, stabbing him in the chest just above his heart. Amrik fell backwards because of the impact and the weight of the fighter.

He rolled over before the fighter could pounce on him again. The fighter hit the ground and winced in pain. Amrik rolled back in a flash and sat on the fighter's back, with his left leg around his neck and the knee of his right leg behind his neck, holding him in a stranglehold akin to a Shimewaza hold.

The LTTE fighter lay almost paralysed under him but still tried to swing his bayonet. Amrik, with all his strength, cut at the fighter's right hand as he swung and severed the wrist from the hand. The fighter screamed with all the strength he had left, and this time, he could be heard over the din of the firing bullets.

Amrik was feeling faint. His head was getting lighter and the sound of the firing was fading.

He was still sitting on the LTTE fighter.

'*Nischey kar apni jeet karoon*', he whispered through the blood that was now flowing out of his own mouth, and with one smooth movement of his right hand, he moved the Kirpan across the fighter's neck. The pressure of the jugular vein, JVP in medical terms, is enough to throw the blood 18 inches when severed. In the LTTE fighter's case, it may have gone beyond that.

Amrik rolled over, the loss of blood now making him weak and drowsy. He stood up unsteadily and returned his

Kirpan to its sheath. He started walking back to his LMG position to take on the next wave of LTTE fighters. He could see them moving in closer from the alleys. An LTTE sniper perched on one of the rooftops sighted Amrik and pressed the trigger. The bullet pierced his chest and he sank.

'*Wahe Guru*…', and then darkness fell.

The situation at Jaffna university was getting more precarious by the minute. Biru was now moving from man to man, repeating his instructions to keep digging and hold the LTTE fighters at bay. It was a losing battle, and he knew it by now. It would be impossible for him to hold on after suffering so many casualties. With no orders to abandon the DZ, he had to hold on until the end—*until the last man, with the last bullet.*

***

The three Para Commandoes teams were now well entrenched in the three houses that they had taken over.

Every time the LTTE fighters tried to move in, accurate and intense fire from these positions compelled them to move back and carry away their casualties with them.

Back at the Div HQ, information was pouring in from all the positions. The situation was getting precarious and Harkirat knew that the Para Commandoes were holed up in the huts. They would not be able to maintain their positions for too long.

'Hoshiyar', he addressed the Col GS, 'Get Tiger 1st Maratha LI on the line. Tell him to establish contact with the Commandoes and provide 81mm mortar fire support to ease the pressure on them. Maybe then they will be able to break out from their present positions. I am fearful that the LTTE may overwhelm them soon'.

The 1st Maratha unit was located inside Jaffna Fort, which was in the heart of the town, and had been encircled by the LTTE for the last ten days. The area was strewn with booby traps, mines, and ambushes, and was surrounded by a hostile population; there was no way he could have broken out through them.

He was waiting impatiently for the columns of 13 Sikh LI and 4/5 GR to reach his location and break the encirclement when he received the instructions from Hoshiyar.

'Roger Sir', the CO replied.

'One Mike for Ten Papa, pass coordinates of your position', the OP officer passed the message to Sheonan on the radio set.

'Golf Romeo (Grid Reference) 412916, I say again, Golf Romeo 412916, Oscar Tango 35 degrees', Sheonan passed the longitude, latitude, and the angle of the target from his position to the Mortar position officer.

The mortars moved quickly, and the guns were set according to the details passed by him.

'*Ek* (One) round, ranging fire', ordered the OP officer.

'Bombs *gaye, uran ka samay char-saat* second', the Mortar position officer said into the radio set, indicating that the ranging bomb had been fired and the flight time was forty-seven seconds.

Sheonan and the teams waited in anticipation, holding their breath to see the impact.

The round fell about 300 metres ahead of Sheonan's position.

'*Niche do sau* (down 200)', Sheonan gave the correction to the officer.

The Mortar officer made the cardinal mistake of skipping a second ranging shot and passed the orders to the mortar position. He plotted the correction on the plotter and gave orders.

'*Teen* round *tez* mortar fire (three rounds rapid fire)', he said.

The rounds fell nowhere near the group of LTTE fighters, but tragically, two rounds landed in the veranda of the hut where Ranjit's team was holed up, killing two commandoes instantaneously and severing the torso of Havildar Dhan Singh.

Two other commandoes rushed out from inside the room to evacuate him.

'It is no use trying to help me', he said.

Before they realised what was happening, he shot himself with his 9mm browning pistol.

'STOP FIRE!', Sheonan yelled into the radio set, halting the Mortar officer, but the damage had been done.

The LTTE fighters, apprehensive that more mortar bombs may follow, moved back, although they still kept firing at the huts. This gave the teams some time to readjust their defensive positions.

***

At the DZ, the firefight was getting deadlier. The strength of Biru's platoon was dwindling, and a sense of despair and panic was taking over the handful of soldiers who were still battling to keep the LTTE fighters at bay. They were coming in waves, firing from their AKs, SLRs, and CMGs. Biru thought for a moment that their weapons, other than the AKs, looked so similar to those issued by the Indian Army.

He was on the right flank of his makeshift defence, with an LMG group directing fire. The eight soldiers who remained, including Biru, had closed in and taken up an all-around defensive position as the LTTE fighters had surrounded them. Bullets flew from every possible direction, including the rooftops. Biru was convinced that it was a matter of time before they were overwhelmed by the LTTE fighters. They were low on ammunition and the unopened ammunition boxes lay in the area now captured by the LTTE.

***

Mahattaya and Yogi were still on the terrace of the university building, directing the operations with military finesse. They had mobilised their reserve fighters from the villages nearby. Kids on bicycles were sent from door-to-door to instruct the fighters to reach the battle zone. The senior fighters were directing them either to the DZ or to where the Para Commandoes were. Hundreds of LTTE fighters were pouring into the DZ.

'I think it is time for the Supremo to move out of this place', Yogi told Mahattya who crouched beside him.

'I agree, more troops will come in, and then it may not be feasible', he replied.

'Anna, we have been attacked by the IPKF and they are coming in large numbers. We must get out of here before it becomes untenable for us. Even now, we may have to fight our way through', he cautioned Prabhakaran.

Prabhakaran took the handset of the radio next to him, and spoke into it in Tamil, 'We have been surrounded by the IPKF and there are slim chances that I may get through. This may be my last message to all of you. Best of luck. *Tamil Ellanukku*', Prabhakaran concluded, bidding goodbye to his cadres.

They moved out of the university building amidst the heavy fire that was coming in from Biru's team. The soldiers had shifted closer to the building and a few waited along its walls.

Mahattaya instructed his fighters to start creating a safe corridor for them to leave the university campus.

A few of the LTTE fighters rushed the four Sikh LI soldiers who were at the entrance of the building. The soldiers kept firing at the LTTE fighters downing six of them before emptying their magazines. The LTTE fighters realised this because suddenly all firing from the soldiers stopped, and as the fighters moved ahead firing ferociously, there was no retaliatory fire from the soldiers. It took them just a few minutes to kill the soldiers and establish a safe passageway for Anna.

Prabhakaran, with Mahattaya and Yogi, left the Jaffna university campus at about 0200 hours. A Datsun pick-up van took them south into Jaffna town.

The town was well fortified, and all approaches to it were strewn with IEDs. Pre-designated ambush sites that could be occupied within minutes and adjusted according to the fluidity of the battle, had been earmarked. Sniper positions on rooftops were occupied around the clock. Prior to the induction of the IPKF, the LTTE had beaten back a full-fledged offensive by the SLAF and had bloodied its defences and fighters.

Prabhakaran was confident that he would leave the IPKF with a bloody nose too, if they dared to attempt an offensive on Jaffna. This would be proven right in the future.

As he drove past the town, he was happy to see it secure. In the past few years, nearly all of the Sinhalese population had migrated from the town and peninsula to the south for their safety. Tell-tale signs of the vicious and bloody battle fought with the SLAF were still evident along the streets. Damaged and burnt houses and debris from factories and other buildings told the story of the days and nights of the past war.

'What is the latest news from the university?', he asked Yogi.

'A few left, it will not be long before they are dead too', he replied.

'Haven't they held on for a longer duration than we thought they would?', Prabhakaran questioned.

'Yes, although just a handful of them remain, they are fighting bravely. I also saw their officer moving from soldier to soldier, motivating them to stick on and fight', Mahattaya replied.

'Hmm...', Prabhakaran said thoughtfully.

***

At the DZ, the eight men in the defensive position had been reduced to five.

'Gore', Biru said to Sepoy Gora Singh who was to his right, 'take the 2-inch mortar, and with Sepoy Hariman, move to your right and fire high explosive rounds (HE) at the advancing LTTE', Biru indicated to the ditch that was about 20 feet from where they stood.

'Yes Sir', Gora Singh replied, and with the 2-inch mortar, he moved to the ditch.

Within minutes, the 2-inch mortar HE rounds started scattering the attack that the LTTE fighters were building up.

Biru, with the other sepoy, was still holding on to their position behind a few coconut trees but they could see the LTTE fighters closing in.

Now nearly out of ammunition, Biru changed his firing change lever to a single shot and waited for the LTTE fighters to come really close before he fired at them. He wanted to make each round count.

'Sukhbir!', he shouted, trying to be heard over the sound of heavy firing.

Sukhbir, who was behind a coconut tree next to Biru, did not seem to hear him.

Biru shouted again. There was no response.

He rolled across to reach him. Sukhbir was dead. Slumped against the coconut tree, his body was riddled with bullets.

Biru was alone. Tired and disoriented, he checked his ammunition—just the magazine on the carbine with nothing left in his ammunition pouch. Sukhbir's SLR had a magazine and Biru picked it up. Not a single round in it. Biru searched him for additional magazines but there were no rounds anywhere to be found.

The first two rounds of the AK-47 hit him on his legs and he fell behind a coconut tree. He returned fire, killing the LTTE fighter who was rushing at him.

The next two bullets were of a 7.62mm LMG, more lethal than the AK. They tore his left shoulder apart. He kept firing single shots from his carbine until his magazine was empty.

The numbness has set in and suddenly, he was neither tired nor did he feel the pain of his injuries. The burst of the LMG that hit him on the chest had thrown him on his back. The sky had cleared and the stars shone brilliantly. He lay motionless, staring at the sky and savouring his tranquil surroundings. The cool, light wind and the sound of the stream of rainwater flowing under him took him back many years, to when, as a schoolboy, he had gone on a trek in the mountains and then rested next to a stream at night. The serenity had returned. The darkness enveloped him like the womb, and he felt warm and secure. He was tired and wanted to sleep. Who were these men around him? Why were they keeping him up?

His breathing was now coming in gasps, his heart could no longer pump enough blood to his vital organs as the blood flowing out of the body lowered the pressure. There was silence all around. The LTTE fighters had formed a ring, and silently, everyone paid homage to this valiant soldier who had fought until he shot the last bullet he had.

Gora Singh saw Biru fall and, with him surrounded by the LTTE fighters, he was worried that they may take him alive.

'Sahab has been surrounded by the LTTE, let's get him out of there', he told his two other comrades.

'We have no ammunition Gore, how can we do it?'

'Fix your bayonets', Gore said, adjusting his own.

'*Jo bole so nihal, sat sri akal*', was the terrifying war cry that the LTTE fighters heard in the silence of the night. They had no idea that some of the soldiers were still alive.

The three LTTE fighters who were standing closer to the charging soldiers took the brunt of the fury of the bayonets. The others fired back at the soldiers. Except for Gora Singh, the other two died instantaneously.

Before Gora Singh could turn back towards the charging LTTE fighters, a 2-inch mortar HE round fired by the LTTE burst a few yards from him, killing the LTTE fighter rushing towards him. A splinter cut through his tibial nerve, throwing him to the ground. His head hit the hard surface and he blacked out.

Nadesan, the LTTE commander for Jaffna, walked up to where Gora Singh was lying and told his men, 'I think this man is alive, take him and make sure no one harms him, he will be an asset during the exchange of our fighters. Put him up with the other Indian Army prisoners in our camp'.

Balasingham Nadesan was a close confidant of Prabhakaran and had been recently deployed in Jaffna with his cadre after the LTTE had intercepted the wireless message of the SHBO that was to be undertaken by the IPKF. A tall, well-built Tamilian, Nadesan looked more like a professional boxer than an LTTE fighter. Belonging to a daily-wage earning family, he had been hand-picked by Prabhakaran to join the ranks of the LTTE. He had a sharp mind that could understand tactical battle situations from a bigger perspective and take quick and ruthless decisions. The fear psychosis that he created in the minds of the SLAF and the local population was enough to keep them indoors.

'Tell all the fighters to start moving towards the huts where the Indian paratroopers are holed up. Now, it is their turn to die', he told his deputy.

'We will collect these bodies and burn them in the morning', he continued, indicating the bodies of the dead Sikh LI soldiers.

Gora Singh had been blindfolded and his hands were tied behind his back. The pain in his leg was unbearable but he was thankful that he was alive. He was aware that they were other people, most probably Indian soldiers, in the truck. When asked, they told him that they were from the 7th Mahar Regiment and had been captured in an ambush a little while ago. The presence of the soldiers provided Gora Singh some solace.

After travelling for about an hour, the truck came to a halt and all its occupants, including Gora Singh, were told to dismount. They were then led to a room, their blindfolds removed and hands untied.

It was the small, dark room where the eight of them would be cramped up for another six months until they were exchanged for LTTE prisoners with the IPKF.

The Commandoes are Extricated

Lt Col Dalbir Singh, the CO of the 10 Para battalion, had been stationed at Colombo with a mission to protect the President of Sri Lanka from the LTTE or the radical Marxist Janatha Vimukthi Peramuna (JVP, People's Liberation Front), both of whom were against the accord for different reasons.

In case the SLAF staged a coup, they were supposed to move the President out of Sri Lanka on board INS Viraat, the Indian aircraft carrier now docked on the shore of Colombo. The aircraft carrier had an infantry battalion on board to support the commandoes in case required.

INS Viraat, which meant 'Giant' in Sanskrit, was the flagship of the Indian Navy. It was the only Centaur-class aircraft carrier in the inventory of the Navy. The ship was completed and commissioned in 1959 as the Royal Navy's HMS Hermes and was commissioned into the Indian Navy on 12 May 1987. Since then, it has participated in various exercises and friendly trips around the world.

The aircraft carrier had a ski jump to operate the Sea Harrier aircraft. It also carried eighty lightweight torpedoes. The carrier had the capability to transport commandoes up to 750 troops. During war the ship could carry up to twenty-six combat aircraft and could support amphibious operations and conduct anti-submarine warfare (ASW) operations.

The Commandoes had also been tasked to protect Radio Ceylon, the official radio station of GoSL and the only one they had, against any forceful takeover by the previously mentioned groups.

Dalbir and his team had been staying in a hotel in Colombo for the last few days. He had kept a close watch on the operations taking place in Jaffna, receiving the latest update from Sheonan on the VHF set with the team. Discovering that his company was under siege and holed up in three huts, he knew it could mean disaster and the loss of many lives. He decided to move in and take control of the situation.

Dalbir was a veteran of the three wars that India had fought post-Independence and had executed many special operations. He had just taken over command of the unit in April 1987. Within three months of taking over, he had trained the unit well in the tough terrain of the deserts of Rajasthan, working through scorching temperatures ranging from above 45-55° C. In preparations for the operations in Sri Lanka, the unit had also carried out special ops exercises at Salur in Tamil Nadu as the terrain was akin to the one found in Sri Lanka. He was confident that all these preparations and rehearsals would hold them in good stead during the impending operations on the island.

He took the GOC's permission to fly to Palaly in a Chetak helicopter that was stationed in Colombo for recce purposes. Immediately on landing at the Palaly airfield, he moved with his protection team of four commandoes to the HQ of 72 Infantry Brigade, who were still lying low in the coconut plantations around Urumpirai.

The link-up battalion 4/5 GR, had meanwhile been ambushed by the LTTE fighters near Palaly town, on the Palaly-Vasivalan-Jaffna axis. Despite their reputation of being skilled warriors, the Gurkhas suffered heavy casualties. Again, due to their superior knowledge of the terrain and many years of experience in guerrilla warfare against the SLAF, the LTTE fighters got the better of them.

The column of 13 Sikh LI had still not been able to establish contact with 4/5 GR. Bubbles' radio operator had informed him about the ambush.

Bubbles had ordered the unit to change their direction of movement, and they were now travelling on the Palaly-Urumpirai axis with the aim of getting close enough to flank 4/5 GR, which was now in a quagmire.

4/5 GR had suffered heavy casualties in the sniper fire, and the BFNAs of 13 Sikh LI moved ahead and brought the casualties to safer places to treat them.

The forward movement of 4/5 GR and the HQ of 72 Infantry Brigade, had been stalled. All attempts to outflank or rush the LTTE positions had failed, and all of them dug into their positions for a while.

At 0830 hours the next day the LTTE had withdrawn from their positions and the Brigade commander passed orders to resume the advance along a different axis.

They had hardly moved a few hundred metres when hostile fire started coming in unrelentingly on the leading elements.

Bubbles moved the rear company to the flank thinking that the LTTE may have left their sides unguarded.

Major Mohan's Alpha company moved swiftly and cautiously to the flank. Just when he thought that they were in an advantageous position to take on the LTTE fighters, they hit a hostile HMG firewall. The attack was so intense that the leading scouts of the company fell even before they could locate the enemy positions.

Captain BC Trivedi, the RMO, lost count of the soldier casualties coming into the RAP.

The .50 HMG assault from the build-up was firing at a cyclic rate of over 1000 rounds per minute and every casualty that was being brought into the makeshift RAP in a house, had at least two to three bullets in them. Limbs and other body parts had been shattered and blown apart. Trivedi could only administer first aid to them along with a shot of morphine and move them back to the airfield. This was further depleting the number of soldiers.

***

Brigadier Mishra was surprised to see Dalbir appearing from nowhere and without any previous intimation.

'Nice to see you Dalbir. How is it that you are here?', he asked him, still keeping his head down amidst the hostile sniper fire.

'Sir, part of my company is holed up in three huts near Jaffna university, surrounded by the LTTE fighters. I have to go to link up with them and extricate them before the LTTE overwhelms the soldiers', he replied rather matter-of-factly.

'But there is no way you can move any further from here. The complete area is infested with LTTE snipers and they have defences all along the road axis to Jaffna', Brig Mishra countered.

'I have to go, and for me, that means I will go against all the opposition and the odds. I can always sneak in with four of my men', he replied, then after a pause as if realising the futility of the effort he added, 'But you have a point here, that I do not have a sizable force to break the encirclement of the LTTE'. Dalbir's voice faded away as if he were lost in his thoughts.

***

Major Anil Kaul was furious. He was the Squadron Commander of the tank troop (three tanks), which had been stationed in Palaly for the airfield defence, one of which had landed earlier, and two that landed with him this morning. The GOC, in all his wisdom, had despatched the single tank on the Palaly-Point Pedro axis, for convoy protection. This amounted to blasphemy for a tank man, because it was against the basics of tank warfare to move a single tank, which was why the smallest fighting unit in an Armoured Regiment was a troop, akin to a platoon in an Infantry Battalion.

On landing at the Palaly airfield at 0930 hours on 13 October, he drove up to the Div HQ for further orders, and also to look for his tank and crew as he had not found them on the airfield. He was aghast when he found out that the single tank had been sent independently on a mission.

'I am sorry Sir', he told the GOC, 'this is against the basic teachings of tank warfare. It is suicidal to send a single tank to perform any task, let alone for convoy protection. I am recalling it immediately', he said, sounding rather irritated and annoyed.

Major Anil Kaul was a six-foot-tall, well-built officer, and now, with his hostile body language, he seemed a foot taller. The GOC realised his mistake and looked up at Hoshiyar who, prior to ordering the move, had advised the

GOC against the deployment.

'Hoshiyar, recall the tank immediately.'

By 1100 hours, Kaul had started his move, along with his three tanks, towards HQ 72 Inf Bde.

The Commander heard the sound of the tanks coming closer to his location. Hoshiyar had informed him about their arrival, and the Commander had his ears to the ground, along with Dalbir.

'T-72s Sir', Kaul said proudly. These tanks had recently been inducted into the army, and his was the first regiment to be equipped with them.

'Do they move cross country?', Brig Mishra asked sarcastically.

'If I want them to', Anil replied.

'Well, jokes apart, I want you to move as fast as you can and link up with the platoon of the 13 Sikh LI and the company of the Para commandoes in the vicinity of Jaffna university. Lt Col Dalbir Singh is the CO of 10 Para, and will be moving with you. Also, take one company of 13 Sikh LI with you. Maj Mohan is the company commander', Brig Mishra passed curt orders to Kaul.

'Roger that Sir', Kaul replied.

'Best of luck with your T-72s.'

The T-72 tanks were from the family of the Soviet main battle tanks. It was widely exported by the Soviets and had seen service in forty countries and numerous conflicts.

The first prototype of the T-72 was built as a mobilisation model (to be produced only when mobilisation of the army was ordered in the event of a war) titled 'Project 172' by Uralvagonzavod, a Russian machine building company located in Nizhny Tagil, Russia. It eventually went into production during peacetime as well, by a special decree of the Soviet government.

With the Indian tank MBT Arjun still under development, the Indian govt in the early 1980s decided on a mass purchase of the T-72 tanks. Officers and crews from regiments to be converted in order of priority had been sent to USSR to train on these tanks. They would later form the nucleus of the training teams in India. Maj Anil Kaul was part of that nucleus.

10 PARA CDO

CHAPTER 10

BACK AGAINST THE WALL

It was the morning of 13 October. The LTTE fighters were still holding on to their positions on the outskirts of Urumpirai, and Charlie company of 13 Sikh LI was still trying to push forward, with the support of 4/5 GR on its eastern flank. The snipers were well placed and any exposed movement was proving fatal.

It had been more than six hours and the complete Brigade group had not advanced more than 3 kilometres. The baptism by fire of all these units who had never seen actual combat was proving to be very costly. The fatality and casualties were increasing by the hour and no forward progress was being made.

Bubbles was getting desperate as he imagined the

worst for Biru and his platoon. The head of the advancing column had entered Kokuvil, but now their advance was becoming slower amid heightened opposition from the LTTE fighters who were well entrenched in the houses. Sections and platoons were moving from house to house and street to street, clearing these oppositions. With no training in urban warfare, the soldiers were learning their lessons by suffering casualties.

***

Dalbir was perched on the turret of the T-72 being commandeered by Anil. The other two tanks were moving on the flanks, about 10 to 15 metres on either side. The coconut plantation was dense, and with torrential rain still pouring down, Anil was worried about the tanks getting bogged down in the slush, but with the teams stuck in Jaffna university fighting for their lives, there was not an iota of doubt in his mind about pushing on.

Havildar Pursottam Singh, with his buddy of 10 Para, was walking ahead of the tank column as scouts and warning them of any IEDs or mines on the way. The tanks had to skirt them with utmost caution and deliberation, thereby delaying the operation further. The movement was slow, laborious, and riddled with dangers that could put the entire rescue operation in jeopardy. The forty-odd men who were left of 'company' 13 Sikh LI were following the tanks.

As they approached the south section of Urumpirai, they were greeted with HMG fire. Purshottam and his buddy took cover behind the tanks and identified the elevated concrete overhead water tank about 300 metres to their north that was being used by the LTTE fighter as an elevated fire position to shower bullets on them. Purshottam indicated the target to Anil, who now had his head out of the cupola, and could see the HMG shooter.

Although the HMG round had no effect on the tank, the intense fire was holding up the troops of 13 Sikh LI and could cause casualties. The only option was to take down the concrete water tank along with the HMG. After Anil passed the executive orders to his tank gunner, it took exactly ten seconds for the automatic loader to load the round and the gunner to align the main gun.

'Fire', Anil ordered. The HE round warhead left the barrel of the gun with fire, heat, and smoke. Within seconds, it hit the concrete overhead tank. The warhead exploded, which in turn caused the water tank to explode into thousands of pieces. It looked like a water plume, and when the dust settled, the LTTE fighter and his HMG were nowhere to be seen.

They had just crossed the road coming from Uduvil when another HMG opened fire from a hut in the direction of the Inuvil railway station building. This time, the gunner did not wait for Anil's orders and engaged the target. The building required just two rounds of HE and then there was silence all around.

Major Anil Kaul realised that they were progressing at a snail's pace, and it would be too late by the time they reached the team of commandoes at Jaffna university. The route was strewn with IEDs and there was no way they could ignore them. This hampered their movement and made it dangerous for them when they took detours to avoid the explosives.

'Anil, at this speed I am afraid we may not reach the team in time and they may get overwhelmed by the numerically superior LTTE fighters', Dalbir said anxiously, as if reading his mind.

'I agree with you Sir, you are only confirming my fears. I have been thinking, if I put my tanks on the railway track, it will give us two advantages. One, there will be no IEDs or booby traps on it as they know that we do not use the train, and the train is their only connection with the rest of Sri Lanka. Secondly, it will also be the fastest route into Jaffna. I can see on the tourist map given to me, that the railway line goes straight through the university in Jaffna, and our teams are most probably in the area of the physical education unit on the Aadiyapatham road, here', he said, pointing at the place marked on the map with his finger.

'That's brilliant thinking Anil. Let us go ahead without much ado. We are already behind schedule', Dalbir said gleefully, delighted by the prospect of reaching his team faster now.

The tanks wheeled towards the railway track, got on the ballast, and then over the sleepers and the rails, uprooting the fasteners on the way. They wheeled right to face the route towards Jaffna university. Now both the tracks of the tanks were on the ballast, and the rails in between them. They drove on, full speed ahead.

As they approached the Kondavil village, an LTTE fighter suddenly appeared from behind a clump of coconut trees and fired an RPG rocket at them. He could not have missed the leading tank from about 20 metres and the rocket hit the glacis and exploded. The splinters ricocheted towards the turret. Anil, who had his head outside the cupola, just saw the rocket being fired and then felt a hot tearing sensation on his face. He fell backwards into the tank. Dalbir was lucky as the other splinters missed him by a whisker.

Purshottam had been shot dead by the LTTE fighter.

'Anil, Anil!', Dalbir shouted, looking inside the turret.

'Sahab has been hit on his left eye and ring finger sir,' said the gunner from inside the tank.

Dalbir could see that Anil was bleeding profusely both from his eye and the severed finger.

'Get the first aid kit out and give him a shot of morphine and start bandaging', Dalbir instructed.

Anil was losing blood fast and was slowly slipping into delirium.

By the time they administered the shot of morphine, he was already deeply asleep. The bleeding had stopped and his breathing and pulse were stable, and that is all Dalbir knew about medicine and first aid. He took over command of the tanks and immediately returned to the 13 Sikh LI RAP, depositing Anil there. He then moved back to his mission and kept pushing ahead, despite the isolated sniper fire on the way.

Ranjit first heard the sound of the tank's main gun and he was sure that he was right about the sound. It did not seem too far now, but the LTTE fighters were closing in. They were converging on all sides with overwhelming strength. The commandoes were still keeping them at bay, moving from one firing position to another keeping strict fire control on the limited ammunition with them. The carbines, SLRs, and the 9mm browning pistols were no match for the highly sophisticated and technically superior

AK-47 rifles that the majority of the LTTE fighters were carrying. This, along with the RPGs, grenades, and SLRs that they took from the dead Sikh LI troops, augmented their arsenal far beyond the commandoes. But the superior training, better command and control, the will to survive, and the pride in their outfit, put the commandoes a notch above the overwhelming numerical superiority of the LTTE fighters.

Sheonan and Nair had spread out with their teams to the adjoining huts, to give the LTTE fighters a false impression of their numerical strength and present a bigger frontage to them.

Muruganeshan, the local LTTE commander, also heard the sound of the tank's main gun at the same time that Ranjit must have heard it. He was not sure whether it was a rocket launcher or whether the Indian mortars had started to fire at them again. As the rounds did not land anywhere near him, he presumed that it may be happening somewhere else. But the sound of the .50mm bullet came almost simultaneously with the impact of it on his chest. It blew a clear 8-inch hole at the exit wound that instantly filled up with blood. Muruganeshan took the first bullet fired by the leading tank, from a distance of about 500 metres.

The roar of the engine and the clanking of the track created an atmosphere of shock and awe. The firing of the main and the secondary gun at the same time was devastating, not only in terms of the loss of human lives, but it also had a complete morale-shattering effect on its adversary. That is exactly what happened, as the frontline of the LTTE fighters fell like dry leaves in autumn. The fighters in the coconut plantations were in absolute disarray and the command and control broke down. They ran helter-skelter towards any escape route that they could find, a few of them stumbling to the small outcrops in the fields. Those in the rear were not as lucky and took bullets from the commandoes who had now come out to the courtyard of the huts, firing their remaining ammunition at the scared and fleeing fighters.

Dalbir stopped the tanks about 100 metres short of the huts and signalled Sheonan to collect his team and get them to the tanks.

'How many casualties?', he asked Sheonan as he approached him.

'Nine fatal and twelve injured', he answered, after taking a count from the team commanders.

'Okay, put them on the tanks and let's get out of here as fast as we can, lest the LTTE f*****s get on top of us again', Dalbir said.

'What about the Sikh LI team?', Sheonan enquired.

'What about them?', Dalbir countered.

'I mean, do we plan to go and rescue them?'

'We can', Dalbir paused, 'Do you think they are still alive?'

'No. But we can confirm what has happened to them.'

'The LTTE fighters have regrouped and fresh reinforcements have come in from the adjoining areas. A radio intercept also confirmed that the fighters at the DZ have moved here to join their comrades. This more or less confirms our fears about the fate of the Sikh LI platoon', Ranjit added, rushing in from his position behind a hut.

'Let's get out of here. They are coming in overwhelming numbers and it may become almost impossible to get out if we waste more time', said Dalbir.

The team had counted their dead and injured, and after loading them onto the tanks, started moving back to Palaly airport.

Dalbir was proud of his boys. They were weary, tired, and hungry after fighting a pitched battle for thirty-two hours. He was happy that they had trained hard during peacetime, and now they had repaid it in sweat and blood.

Sheonan suddenly broke the silence between them.

'Sir, do you remember the saying on the board in our training area? "The more you sweat in peace, the less you bleed in war". It was proven true today', he said.

'Yes, Sheonan'

'My chest fills with pride today to see that the boys have upheld the glorious tradition of the unit, and have proven once again that they are the best', he replied.

The team was moving astride the railway track as the tank moved over the tracks. They had moved about a kilometre when they saw Subedar Major Jaswant Singh Rathore with a team of ten commandoes and two 1-tons.

'Jai Hind Sahab', he said saluting Dalbir.

'How are you here SM Sahab?', asked Dalbir.

'Sir, I have come with food for the boys, they have not had anything to eat for the last two days', he replied.

Dalbir looked at Sheonan and smiled. The camaraderie here was something to see.

After a break of about twenty minutes wherein all of them had their fill, the teams resumed their journey towards their destination.

Brigadier Mishra was pleased to see the Para Commandoes returning safely, and so was Bubbles, to have Mohan's Alpha company returned so that operations could progress further.

Anil, along with the other casualties, was evacuated to Palaly airfield, so that necessary medical aid could be provided and the more serious cases could be moved to the Military hospital at Madras.

Mohan gave Bubbles an update on the situation at the

university, and also the fate of the platoon at the DZ.

Bubbles had already presumed the worst for Biru's team but the confirmation hit him hard. Within the first thirty hours of landing in Sri Lanka, the unit had already lost one officer, two JCOs, and forty-two ORs which was a heavy loss by any standards, and as the CO of the unit, Bubbles was devastated.

He got up from the small boulder that he had been sitting on, and started walking and whistling. His buddy walked up to him with a cup of coffee. Sipping on his coffee, he started thinking about Biru, his wife, and their child.

How will I face them?, he thought.

He was still deep in thought when the radio operator informed him that the Commander wanted to speak to him.

The Commander informed Bubbles that the Army Commander had personally conveyed to Harkirat that 13 Sikh LI should be pulled back to Palaly airfield for rest and recoup, as they have been in battle for more than forty-eight hours and had suffered heavy casualties.

Bubbles told the Commander to kindly convey to the Army Commander that 13 Sikh LI would not need rest until it reached Jaffna. He requested he not pass such messages to them as it would have an adverse effect on the morale of the troops.

He also in turn sent a message to the Army Commander on the Bravo One Link.

'From Tiger One-Three (13 Sikh LI) to Tiger India Papa Kilo Foxtrot (IPKF). Unit will not, I repeat, will not return for Romeo and Romeo (Rest and Recoup). Request to allot fresh mission.'

***

It was the morning of October 14, when Nadesan and his group of LTTE fighters came back to the DZ, to pick up the dead bodies of the soldiers of 13 Sikh LI. They piled them up in a hand cart and moved them to the Thalayali Viravavar temple, about a kilometre from the DZ. Prabhakaran, Mahattaya, and Yogi had returned to watch the display of bodies and the weapons captured. It was a big success for the LTTE.

'Now do you see what the LTTE can do? This is how we will kill the Indian soldiers. This is just the beginning, let them dare enter our sacred land and we will kill each one of them', Prabhakaran said, addressing the large crowd that had gathered at the temple ground to watch the spectacle.

'*Tamil Elanukku*', he shouted.

This nationalist speech worked the crowd into frenzied cheering. Prabhakaran was their hero. They believed every word that he spoke, and all the rumours that had been spread to portray him as a larger-than-life figure. If anyone could get them the Tamil homeland—it was Anna.

On 27 July 1973, at the tender age of nineteen, Velupillai Prabhakaran shot and killed A. Duraiappa, the Tamil mayor of Jaffna. This was where one of the most remarkable careers in the international history of guerrilla warfare began. He now had an estimated 10,000-odd armed male and female LTTE fighters, who swore their loyalty to no one other than their commander, a wise old veteran at thirty-seven. They preferred to swallow cyanide rather than be taken captive.

Born into a fisherman's family of the backward Karaivarar caste in Velvettithurai, which was widely known as the smuggler's village in the Jaffna peninsula, Prabhakaran was brought up on a steady dose of stories about the glory of Tamil history. He was so impressed that he often compared himself to the legendary Chola king, Karikalan.

At sixteen, he dropped out of school to launch the Tamil New Tigers (TNT). The choice of that acronym was to prove prophetic as the Tigers grew to become the most consummate explosives experts in the shadowy world of international terrorism.

Prabhakaran was publicity-shy and rarely opened up

to researchers or journalists. His personal charisma and mystique had convinced cadres of the ultimate inevitability of Eelam.

Prabhakaran picked his recruits young, predominantly in the twelve-thirteen range. These children had been born into hardship and grew up witnessing the atrocities of the Sri Lankan soldiers. Their training was completed by an oath of personal loyalty to Prabhakaran and the gift of a cyanide capsule to welcome the new fighter on his behalf. The credo of the Prabhakaran cult was not death-or-glory, it was death-and-glory.

He also had a 3,000-strong women's wing. Skilled in close combat, they formed a part of the LTTE's suicide squad, the Black Tigers. Adele Balasingham, forty-one years of age and the Australian wife of LTTE ideologue Anton, was believed to be the unofficial head of the women's wing.

In the peninsula, the Tigers collected taxes, as any government would. The majority of the lakhs of Sri Lankan Tamils spread across the world preferred to send them money through their LTTE contacts.

In the early 1970s, the United Front coalition, led by Sirimavo Bandaranaike, introduced the Policy of standardisation that made the criteria for university admissions lower for the Sinhalese than for the Tamils. Several organizations were formed by Tamil students, to counter this act. Prabhakaran, then just fifteen years of age, dropped out of school and joined the Kuttimani-Thangathurai group (which later evolved into TELO), formed by Selvarajah Yogachandran (known as Kuttimani) and Nadarajah Thangathurai, both of whom also hailed from Valvettithurai.

Several anti-Tamil policies by successive Sinhalese-majority governments upset Prabhakaran to the extent that he formed his own militant organisation in 1970. After he assassinated the mayor of Jaffna, he announced his entry into the armed struggle movement against the GoSL.

On 5 May 1976, he formally announced the creation of the Liberation Tigers of Tamil Eelam (LTTE), which over the years, had become the most feared and sophisticated terrorist group in the world. It was believed by the R&AW that along with the support that the Indian Government was extending to the LTTE, they had also established contacts with private mercenary groups to train them in military operations including assassinations, sabotage, making and operating IEDs, and deadly ambushes.

By the end of 1983, the LTTE had managed to conjure up a reputation that instilled fear in the hearts of the SLAF and other law and order organisations but love in the hearts of the Tamilians.

Moderate in height but heavily built, he sported a bushy moustache and would only be seen rarely. He was always attired in the LTTE uniform with his trademark 9mm browning pistol.

The R&AW had also got hold of reliable information that his organisation's net worth was upward of 300 million dollars by way of illegal weapons and drug trade, coupled with the donations pouring in from influential Tamilians in other countries.

The crowd was mesmerised whenever they saw or heard him. Today was a victorious day for them. The mighty Indian Army's first operation had ended disastrously and the credit went to Prabhakaran and his fighters.

The mad frenzy reached its zenith when Nadesan poured petrol on the bodies and set them on fire. The crowd and the LTTE fighters were dancing around the pyre.

'*Tamil Elanukku, Tamil Elanukku!*', the sky resounded with the LTTE slogan.

It was a sad end for the brave fighters.

LT COL RS 'BUBBLES' SETHI

CHAPTER 11

I HAVE A MISSION TO ACCOMPLISH

With casualties mounting and only six officers left, Bubbles decided to reorganise his companies to have viable fighting strength in each one of them.

The unit had moved from the ambush site to the Palaly-Jaffna railway line and solidified their position under intermittent sniper fire coming from the direction of Urelu village.

By the evening of 14 October, they decided to clear Urelu and move ahead towards Jaffna.

Luckily for the unit, the two missing companies had joined in and now with enhanced strength, Bubbles was more confident of clearing the opposition at Urelu.

With the tanks also now available to support the attack,

and a BMP along with an engineering company to handle the IEDs, a plan was put into place by Bubbles.

Maj Chhangani with his Bravo company was tasked to lead the attack again, with the remaining unit assigned to follow him.

Charlie company, under Srichand, was to provide the fire support from the present location.

Bubbles distributed the rest of Delta company among the other companies.

Just then, Bubbles received a message again, this time directly from the Army Commander, to pull back to the Palaly airfield for reorganisation and rest.

Bubbles personally spoke to him, and in the most diplomatic and tactful language, rejected the possibility of going back.

'I have a mission to accomplish', he said. 'I will not fall back until it is completed. I request you Sir, please do not pull me back now', he said.

The Army Commander relented.

Urelu is a small town with a population of approximately 2,500. It is located south of Punnalaikkadduvan, west of Achchelu, east of Chunnakam, and north of Urumpirai. The town is spread over an area of 3 square kilometres with banana and tobacco plantations covering large swaths of land. A few houses line the outskirts of the town and the concentration of buildings increase as one moves into the centre of the settlement. The town is well laid out with lanes and by-lanes clearly demarcating the area.

Being strategically placed geographically, it was imperative to clear Urelu in order to move ahead towards Jaffna. The LTTE was well-entrenched and had taken up defensive positions in the houses. The Palaly-Jaffna road passed through this town and for the other military elements to be moved, it had to be cleared and secured.

Bubbles explained this to his 'O' group. The aim was not to get into a pitched battle but to use maximum force to clear the axis and move ahead. Other following units would clear the LTTE opposition in detail. Bubbles aimed to maintain speed and reach the university as quickly as possible.

He decided that he would launch the attack sometime around dusk. It would give him the added advantage of some daylight and orientation by the time the battle was set in motion. In the meantime, the troops would have also settled into the area.

Another impediment in their planning was the delay in the fetching up of the unit's F echelon vehicles.

These F Echelon vehicles consisted of the personnel, vehicles, and equipment required by the units to fight the battle, and included a mix of fighting and command, control, and communication systems elements required to plan and conduct operations.

As the unit had moved with only a part of the first line ammunition, which is how infantry units generally moved, and with hardly any time to open and charge the magazines, a large section of their resources remained in the F Echelon. The road from Palaly to Urelu had to be cleared and secured for the F echelon vehicles to move. 4/5 GR in the rear had secured parts of the road, but there were still places where the LTTE snipers were holed up and had stalled the convoy.

The complete ammunition was usually divided into three parts—first, second, and WWR. The first line was carried when moving into battle, with the second line being fetched up as and when required, or when there was a lull in the battle. The War Wastage Rate ammunition kept the second line replenished, which in turn did the same for the first line ammunition.

By evening, the unit was prepared for the attack on Urelu.

Srichand's Charlie was leading the attack. His company would wheel east from its present location and approach Urelu from the west. The leading platoon commander had been instructed by Srichand, to capture at least three to four houses, so that they could establish a foothold and build on it, forming a firm base to further the operations into Urelu.

It was becoming extremely difficult to distinguish between the LTTE cadres and the civilians. Unlike the Sikh LI officers and soldiers, who stood out because their uniforms and turbans indicated they were non-Tamils, the LTTE cadre wore *lungis* and *baniyans* akin to the civilians, which was the traditional clothing of the Tamils. With no weapon on a Sri Lankan Tamilian, he would appear to be an innocent civilian.

It was easy for the LTTE snipers to pick up the officers and radio operators, whom they had been instructed to eliminate. Among the Sikh soldiers, the officers stood out like a sore thumb, and their slouch hats made them conspicuous among the turbans. The IPKF learnt this after suffering many officer casualties. The radio operators were picked up by the snipers for obvious reasons—to disrupt the communications. They were easily identifiable because of the big ANPRC 25A radio set on their backs. The operators also gave away the officer's positions as they would usually be next to the radio operators, for easier access to the radio set.

The assault went off as planned. With the two tanks leading the attack, the initial phase of capturing a few huts on the outskirts of the village was a cakewalk. The IPKF was still in their initial learning phase and walked into the LTTE's well-laid trap. The LTTE fighters held their fire and did not expose their locations. The villagers were still occupying their houses, which was part of the LTTE plan, as this slowed down the advance and no speculative fire could be brought upon the houses.

But as the tanks moved ahead and the leading element of Srichand's Charlie moved in, the LTTE opened up a heavy volume of fire from the ambushes that they had laid. Srichand was surprised to see that women and children were out in the streets and the LTTE fighters were firing from behind them. His soldiers were holding fire and waiting in anticipation for Srichand's orders. It was something that neither he nor the IPKF had ever witnessed. He could not order firing on women and children but his company was taking casualties. He had to think and think fast to get over this precarious situation. He was also fully aware that the soldiers would not hold fire for too long now. Seeing their comrades fall, they would open fire on the civilians, and then it would be almost impossible to stop them. He shouted, 'Hold fire. No one will fire until I open fire'.

'Sir, we have already suffered two fatal casualties and our positions are exposed. The LTTE snipers will pick and shoot at us', said Tejbir Singh, the senior JCO of the company.

'I know that, but we have to also understand that innocent civilians are being used as human shields. The LTTE wants us to open fire on them so that it makes heart-rendering news in the west and maligns the IPKF's reputation. If we do not, then we suffer casualties. This is a precarious situation Tejbir Sahab, but a decision has to be taken. What is your opinion on this?', Srichand asked.

Tejbir opened his mouth to speak when a sniper's bullet hit the left of his neck and exited from the right, shattering it. Tejbir, who was on his knees, just slumped.

'Charlie company, FIRE', shouted Srichand and opened fire from his carbine.

The volume of fire when a platoon is firing on unarmed civilians with automatic weapons is a scene no one will want to witness. Some of them were just cut into two pieces by the LMG fire. The 7.62mm light machine gun is a very lethal weapon. Handled by a crew of two soldiers, it can fire up to an average of 500 rounds per minute, travelling at a muzzle velocity of 1200 feet per second. The crowd was at about 20-30 metres, and the bullets did not spread at this distance.

As a few of them fell, and the shrieks of pain and shock overtook the quietness of the night, Srichand just froze for a few seconds. He had never thought of such a scenario even in his weirdest dreams.

The crowd had scattered; a few were picking up the dead and wounded. The snipers had fled, abandoning their positions.

The BFNAs were providing first aid to the injured and moving the dead towards the rear.

'Satpal', Srichand called out to one of the BFNAs, 'There are casualties among the civilians also, give them first aid'.

Satpal looked a little confused at the orders.

'But Sir…', he started.

'Do as I say. They have been used by the LTTE and we have to be humane to them. We had to open fire to save ourselves but they have suffered because of no fault of theirs. They must be helped. Is that understood by all?', Srichand said, addressing his troops.

'Yes, Sir', they replied in unison.

During this lull, one of the platoons took a detour and went into another lane to get behind the ambush. The lane was just about 10 feet wide and had either a wall or barbed wire fencing on both sides, which was the boundary wall of the houses. As the platoon entered the lane, the second ambush opened up fire. Now, this took them completely by surprise. The concept of multiple ambushes was not known to the Indian Army then. The platoon already had seven dead and four injured, in the first barrage of LTTE fire.

The tanks that had moved into the lanes earlier had been caught up due to an IED blast under a culvert, and with the lanes being very narrow they could not turn around.

Srichand was desperately trying to push ahead, but with mounting casualties and his company under heavy fire from all sides, he informed Bubbles that his move ahead had been stalled and he needed someone to release the pressure on him.

Mohan moved ahead and his rocket launcher detachments started taking down the LTTE fighters from their locations. But the fighters were clever and well-trained. The additional advantage, of knowing the terrain well and having the support of the locals, turned them into ghosts. They were appearing, disappearing, and re-appearing from all sides. The darkness had set in, and the soldiers were completely disoriented. Scared that they may get lost or be kidnapped by the LTTE fighters, they bunched together and presented themselves as large targets.

Bubbles had also moved up amidst the chaos and was pushing the soldiers to move ahead. With dead and screaming wounded soldiers lying on the roads, it was an eerie sight for the first-timers, who made up nearly 99 per cent of the soldiers present.

It took Bubbles a while to get them moving. Charlie company had skirted the first few houses and had married up with the tanks. They kept moving ahead behind the cover of the tanks and did not get involved in clearing the resistance pockets as they posed no challenge to the advancing tanks.

Mohan's Alpha moved along two lanes, thereby reducing the risk of a double ambush. The third platoon of Alpha moved a little distance behind the leading ones, with an aim to move in as support to either when necessary.

The unit was learning quickly and adapting to counter the LTTE fighters. The subsequent ambushes were not as deadly as the first one, and the countermeasures by 13 Sikh LI proved very effective.

Srichand was moving at the head of his company, intending to get out of the built-up area that had them boxed up. The LTTE fighters would appear at turnings, from behind the cover of the boundary walls, and fire at the advancing column. Just when the head of Charlie company was nearing the last few houses of Urelu, two LTTE fighters, one with an LMG firing from his hip, and another with an AK-47, appeared from behind the boundary wall of a house. Again boxed up between boundary walls, the head of the company was unable to take up any defensive positions. They retaliated with all their guns blazing. An AK-47 bullet grazed Srichand's left shoulder and it started bleeding profusely. Undeterred, he kept firing and moving ahead, along with the leading elements of his company. The hail of bullets caught the LTTE fighters before they could do any more human damage. They lay dead when the scouts of the company reached them. In the ambient light, Srichand's radio operator saw the wound on his company commander's shoulder and called for the BFNA.

Srichand took out his first field dressing (FFD) from his knapsack and tore it to apply it to his wound. His radio operator also took his out but Srichand told him that one would suffice. The BFNA reached his side and applied the FFD.

An FFD or battle dressing is a kind of bandage carried by soldiers in battle or training, for immediate use in case of gunshot wounds. It consists of a large pad of absorbent cloth, attached to the middle of a strip of thin fabric, used to bind the pad in place. It is used when stopping the bleeding is the top priority. Owing to its unique design of dressing, it can be applied by an injured soldier himself, and with one hand.

With the dressing done and the LTTE opposition silenced for the time being, the company started its move ahead.

News had started pouring in that 4/5 GR had been caught in a deadly ambush on the outskirts of Maruthanandam. One company of 13 Sikh LI under Mohan rushed to relieve the pressure on them. During these two days of fighting the unit had already lost two officers and seventeen soldiers; the number of injured was much higher.

As Mohan reached the location of the ambush, he saw the unit trying to break through the ambush and move across the road where a few casualties lay, but the LTTE snipers in the ambush would not let even a leaf move. Any movement brought accurate sniper fire, which was the reason behind the heavy casualties.

Mohan moved forward to a Second Lieutenant whom he recognised as Raj Sinha, who he had met along with his CO Lt Col IS Bawa just a day earlier. Both of them had come with a company to escort the tanks, but the plans changed and a company of 13 Sikh LI went with the tanks instead.

'Raj, where is the CO?', Mohan enquired.

'Sir, he has been hit and is lying across the road, we have already lost two officers and eleven men trying to rescue him. Even if you lift your head they fire, and I promise, it is absolutely accurate', Raj replied.

Mohan did not want to prove the authenticity of his statement.

He moved ahead with Raj Sinha, to the road where the bleeding casualties lay. It was a tragic sight to see. The snipers were effectively engaging any movement by the

Gurkha soldiers. Mohan could see the CO and his radio operator both lying grievously wounded across the road, amidst a coconut grove. He had been there now for four hours, and the situation was getting perilous.

'We have to get him out from there', Mohan said when he met the leading company commander of the unit.

'Yes, but how?', he asked in desperation.

'I, along with a company of yours, will provide a barrage of covering fire. We will put in all we have. You move in and evacuate the injured or move them to a safer place. The total time we can give you will be five minutes of the barrage. Rush and evacuate. Make the teams now, and nominate who will evacuate whom', Mohan said finally as he laid out the plan.

When the barrage of cover fire started, it was as if all hell had broken loose. Rockets, MMGs, LMGs, 2-inch mortars, and rifle fire rained down. Every weapon was put into it with maximum firepower.

Snipers in both known and unknown positions were engaged for those three minutes. The evacuation teams rushed across the road under the covering fire and started the evacuation drills. The CO and his radio operator were moved first and brought to where Mohan and Raj were located.

The RMO of the unit hopelessly tried to revive the CO, but he had lost too much blood and did not respond.

13 Sikh LI had cleared Urelu and had secured the area for the 5 Parachute Regiment to pass through. Under the cover of the night, the unit silently prowled through the now secure streets of the town and commenced their move towards Urumpirai, the only major town between the advancing columns of IPKF and Jaffna University.

The attack on Urumpirai was to be conducted by 5 Para with 13 Sikh LI in reserve, on the night of 15-16 October. In the last seventy-two hours, the unit had just advanced 6 kilometres. They had another 9 to Jaffna University and 11 kilometres to Jaffna. With each step, the LTTE resistance was increasing, and with mounting casualties on their side, Bubbles was getting increasingly worried about their operation.

5 Para had been reassigned to 72 Inf Bde to fill in for 4/5 GR, which had been pulled back to Palaly for rest and refit. In the ambush, the unit had lost its CO and four officers, with a large number of casualties among the soldiers.

Urumpirai was a large town and was divided into four cardinal parts—east, west, north, and south Urumpirai. It spread over an area of about 8 sq kms. With the area densely populated, it was decided that 5 Para would secure and open the road axis towards Jaffna. The clearing of the town could be done later by follow-up units. As it is, at this moment, they did not have the troops to do it.

It had started raining heavily again, and all timed plans for the attack went haywire. Nonetheless, Bubbles wanted the attack to go in, thereby utilizing the surprise factor that the inclement weather would give them.

5 Para attacked Urumpirai LTTE positions boldly, taking on accurate fire from the fighters. Initially, the LTTE gave away their positions, and as planned, fell back to pre-prepared delaying positions, channelising the 5 Para troops into a pre-selected killing area. Gaining this success whetted the soldiers' appetite for more, and throwing caution to the winds they moved into the trap laid by the LTTE. Within minutes, they were surrounded, and the rear company was cut off from the rest of the unit.

Outnumbered and outgunned, the company fought for their lives and sent out distress signals to the unit ahead. The LTTE fighters had placed themselves between the unit and this company and severed the connection between them. With the LTTE firing at them from all directions and launching assault after assault in small parties, they were like ghosts who could be heard but not seen. There was no way the CO of 5 Para could dispatch reinforcements for the beleaguered company. He sent a message to the Cdr of 72 Inf Bde to relieve the pressure on his company.

Bubbles had no choice but to direct Charlie to move to assist the company of 5 Para. Srichand got the company together from their defensive positions and commenced his move to reach the besieged troop at the earliest. In the last few days, he had learnt that the LTTE fighters would overwhelm the company of 5 Para due to sheer numbers and intimate knowledge of the terrain.

The move along the road was faster than he had expected, as this area had been secured. When he reached the location of 5 Para, he could see the LTTE fighters were spread out on three sides and had the company trapped inside. He immediately moved one platoon to the east and another to the west, to outflank the LTTE positions. When they opened fire, the LTTE knew that they had been outmanoeuvred and left their positions, moving to subsequent delaying positions as they had done previously, leaving behind their dead and wounded.

Only the western edge of Urumpirai had been captured by now, and it had taken them about twelve hours to do so. With the troops exposed to daylight, it became easier for the LTTE snipers to pick and choose their targets. Casualties were mounting on the IPKF side, as they had no cover to save themselves. They entered the houses that were in the area, but they were either hostile or few and far between. 5 Para, with sheer determination and raw courage, kept inching forward, clearing room to room from house to house.

Bubbles was moving with his leading company just a few notches behind, capitalising on the gains made by 5 Para.

By 23 October, the road axis to Urumpirai had been cleared and secured.

The festival of Diwali had come and gone without anyone realising it, and even if someone had he did not mention it to anyone. It had been twelve days since the offensive against the LTTE had started with an aim to capture Jaffna. As per the original plan, Jaffna was to be captured in seventy-two hours. What a joke, Bubbles thought.

It is known in military teachings, that even the best of plans can get thrown out of the window the moment the first bullet is fired. This is exactly what happened during the capture of Jaffna. The only difference here was that there was no plan. It was just flamboyance, callousness, and blind ambition.

Bubbles met the Cdr 72 Inf Bde on the morning of the twenty-third and insisted that his unit be tasked with the capture of Kokuil and Jaffna university. The Cdr was hesitant because the unit was not at full strength, and he feared that on seeing the massacre of their platoon at the university, they would go berserk.

'Bubbles, I think another unit from 118 Inf Bde must

be tasked for the capture of Kokuvil and the university. It may not be correct to task your unit and you know why', Brig Mishra said.

'Sir, I fully understand your hesitancy in tasking me, but I assure you that my troops will maintain all military ethics during the operation. You must understand the effect it will have on their morale when they capture the university. It will be a kind of emotional tribute to the fallen heroes', Bubbles pleaded.

'Okay, if you can assure me that there will be no human rights violations, no civilian casualties, no retribution, and no revenge-seeking, then I will let you undertake this operation, although I know that you are under-strength too.'

'I have been under strength since we left Gwalior, and for the last twelve days, my unit has been used in all operations and has also had to reinforce a few other teams. So bringing up this under-strength issue now is not prudent Sir. In so far as upholding the ethics of war is concerned, I assure you I will not disappoint you', Bubbles replied.

'Well then, make a plan and God speed', the Cdr replied, shaking Bubbles' hand.

The area of Kokuvil was the doorway to Jaffna, and that is where the university campus was situated. As the advancing columns approached Kokuvil, the density of houses, huts, kitchen gardens, plantations, shops, roads, lanes, and by-lanes crisscrossing each other kept increasing steadily to make the area look like a maze of cobwebs woven intricately to confuse.

Without maps or guides, it was becoming increasingly difficult to maintain their direction. Mohan, with the leading company, maintained a steady pace waiting for the ever elusive enemy to strike.

Early in the morning on 25 October, the enemy did finally strike and they struck with impunity. The leading company of 13 Sikh LI was completely pinned down. The LTTE fighters were everywhere. The snipers, ambushes, and fighters trying to rush them with overwhelming strength were not new to them. They had, in the last fortnight, mastered the art of guerrilla warfare, and Bubbles was glad to see the steady progress the unit was making.

Major Chhangani was moving on the western flank, with Mohan on the main axis and Srichand on the eastern flank. The lanes and by-lanes also gave them the flexibility of switching troops from one axis to another if the need arose. Chhangani's leading section suddenly came under heavy HMG fire from one of the houses to their east. The section commander Hav Devinder Singh, along with two soldiers, started crawling towards the house and the LMG detachment of the section took up position to cover them with automatic fire. The rocket launcher also was moved ahead by Chhangani, who had by now moved up to the section.

The 4-foot boundary wall posed an obstacle for the rocket launcher detail to take a direct shot at the firing HMG of the LTTE, as the rockets were hitting above the location where it was positioned. This did not deter the three advancing men, who crawled and took up positions behind the boundary wall. The covering fire from the LMG and the section had kept the LTTE fighter's head down for a while. Suddenly, around ten LTTE fighters rushed in from a by-lane, towards the leading section that was providing the cover fire. Behind them, Chhangani could see a larger group running toward them. The section, now under intense fire with a likelihood of getting overrun, shifted their attack towards the rushing LTTE fighters. Hav Devinder and his team were now without any covering fire and the HMG had started firing at the section, resulting in casualties. He had to act decisively and quickly to save his comrades. He instructed his teammates to cover his move towards the HMG. He took out two hand grenades from his pouch and took off the pins, holding on tightly to the release clips.

The distance from his position to the HMG was just 15 feet now.

'Cover my move', he told his teammates.

Before they even understood the orders, he jumped

over the boundary wall, rushing towards the HMG. The LTTE fighters had shifted their fire and attention towards the section that was being rushed by the other group of fighters.

They only saw Devinder rushing towards them when he had released the clips of the four-second fuse of the hand grenades. He pushed the door of the house open with his shoulder and jumped on the HMG shooters. Two high explosive grenades exploding simultaneously caused a sympathetic explosion of the HMG ammunition and a few IEDs that were stored near the gun.

The gun fell silent and so did Devinder.

With the HMG silenced, the leading section rushed to the advancing LTTE fighters who were taken by surprise. They had never expected the Indian soldiers to counter rush them. In all the earlier encounters the Indians had fought conventionally, holding on to their positions and trying to beat back the attacking LTTE fighters. This was the first time they adopted the same LTTE tactics to counter them. The fighters stopped dead in their tracks not knowing what to do. This was enough time for the Charlie troops to overwhelm them. Not one of the LTTE fighters survived. They fell like nine pins.

Chhangani moved his platoons closer now, as the LTTE opposition was thinning out and he could see them retreating towards Kokuvil. He did not want to break contact with them, not only because he intended to annihilate them, but also because they would act as guides and inadvertently take him to Kokuvil and Jaffna.

Bubbles was keeping himself abreast with the situation through the advancing columns. He moved Mohan and his company just behind Chhangu and told them to prepare for the attack on Jaffna university.

It was 1900 hours when he got his O group together in a temple, on the outskirts of Kokuvil. The university was just 2 kilometres from their location. The temple complex was well laid out, with a boundary wall about 7 feet high and entry and exit doors at opposite ends. The floor was covered with large, red stone tiles, roughly cut and loosely fitted. The sanctum sanctorum was in the centre with a verandah all around. This was about 3 feet above floor level. Wooden carved doors and thick round pillars supported the sloping roof of the temple. By the look of it, it was evident that the temple was the main shrine in the area and had a large number of offerings.

The weather had turned hostile again and the torrential rain was playing havoc. With the countryside infested with LTTE snipers and the roads, lanes, and by-lanes dotted with IEDs and mines, Bubbles had called in his O group to the temple.

'Gentlemen, I am aware that all of you are raring to go ahead with the capture of Jaffna university', he began.

'Believe me, I am as eager to go in as you all are, if not more. But let's plan in detail because we are now at the gates of Jaffna and the LTTE will put in all their might to stop us from getting in. The capture of Jaffna university will give us two advantages. One, we would have avenged the killing of our brothers, and two, the university will act as a firm base for further ops, and subsequently can be converted into an administrative base. Therefore, the operation has to be deliberate and well-coordinated', he said, laying out the introduction to his plan.

'Sir, our 81mm mortars are presently out of range and will not be able to support our attack on the university', Mohan informed.

'So move them up first thing in the morning with 4/5 GR, which is coming in from Palaly after their rest and refit. They can take up positions in this general area and support the attack. Kindly coordinate all details and let me know the fire plan', Bubbles said.

It was to be a two-pronged attack, with the two BMPs leading each company prong. With the mortars providing close supporting fire, it was expected that the LTTE fighters' heads would be kept down until the companies closed in on the positions held by them.

After a foothold was established by either of the companies, the reserve company being led by Srichand was to go through the foothold and start room-to-room and floor-to-floor clearing of the university building. It was estimated that at least sixty to seventy LTTE fighters were within the well-fortified defences in the building.

It was still raining in the early hours of October 24 when the attack commenced. As always, the op did not go as it was planned.

The leading BMPs got bogged down in the slush caused by the heavy rains, and their advance became slow and laborious. They were drawing more fire from the adjacent houses and huts than from the university. Being in the open football ground that had been earlier used by the heliborne forces, the advancing companies feared the same fate.

The fire plan made by Mohan proved to be the saving grace and with the 13 Sikh LI mortar platoon augmented with the mortar platoon of 4/5 GR, the firing of the mortars was very accurate and intense. This broke the will of the LTTE fighters as they suffered heavy casualties and their defences were in disarray.

Under this intense covering fire, the companies crept closer to their objective, moving through ankle-deep slush and the cover of darkness that had fallen after a day-long battle.

Bubbles had hoped that the foothold he had planned could be established before first light so that troops would not be caught in the open. It was already 0540 hours and in about twenty minutes it would be first light. They had been trying to establish a foothold for more than twenty-four hours now.

Chhangu's leading platoon reached the edge of the university building, closing in on the rooms on the western side. The rocket launcher detail fired four rockets at the room closest to them from where an LMG was firing at them. The HE rounds blew two big holes in the wall and silenced the LMG. The leading section assaulted the position and moved inside the building.

The time was 0545 hours.

'Tiger-1 for Tiger-15 over', Bubbles radio set crackled.

'15 for 1 pass your message, over', Bubbles replied in anticipation.

'Lal Gulab, I say again, Lal Gulab', Chhangu emphasised, repeating the code word for the successful completion of phase one of the operation.

'Well done, firm in and consolidate your position. Can you move further?'

'Affirmative', Chhangu replied.

Chhangani's company started clearing the rooms one after another, and there was not much resistance from the

LTTE fighters. They either surrendered or fought without much resistance.

Mohan had also entered the building from the other side and was making steady progress.

By 1000 hours, it was clear that the LTTE had retreated towards the town of Jaffna, where they had better-coordinated defences and planned to give the IPKF a pitched battle.

The university finally fell and was completely cleared and captured by 13 Sikh LI at 1100 hours on 24 October 1987.

Bubbles moved out of the university building, looking for the remnants of his fallen comrades. He was aware that they would not find anyone alive but he wanted some closure to their sacrifice.

The rain had stopped and the sun was now shining brightly on the water-soaked road and the football ground that had been the LZ for his ill-fated platoon.

Bubbles could only see some burnt pieces of the Indian Army uniform and the shoulder titles of his regiment. At one location, at the rear of the university building, he found more of such burnt pieces, along with half-burnt tires and empty jerry cans. He knew what the LTTE had done to his men.

He was filled with mixed emotions. He was raging

with anger and wanted to avenge the brutal killing of his men. He was angry at himself for having succumbed to the orders of the GOC. He was upset about how his men had met their end. He was feeling helpless that he had not been able to link up with them in time.

He was then joined by Mohan and a few officers and soldiers. They all walked slowly towards the Thalayali Viravavar Temple where the bodies of his soldiers had been burnt. It was a heart-rendering site even for the battle-hardened soldiers.

The courtyard in front of the temple was now strewn with half-burnt uniforms and shoulder titles of the Sikh LI regiment. Bubbles, like the others, was simmering with anger. It was becoming more and more difficult for him to control his emotions but the responsibility of controlling his men weighed heavily on him. He knew that one wrong move by him could lead to a massacre of the civilian population around them.

Regaining his demeanour he said, 'Let not their sacrifice be wasted. Let us all pledge that we will, in all ways, avenge the manner in which they have been brutally killed by the LTTE. But we will not touch the unarmed and will treat them with honour and kindness, for we are the Indian Army and we are Sikhs. Remember, it is only the favoured ones who get to lay down their lives on the battlefield. Martyrdom or *shaheed* is the fundamental institution of Sikhism. Bhai Taru Popat was also set on fire by Babar the Mughal king when he spoke against him. Many Gurus have laid down their lives for the Panth. The tenth Guru, Guru Tegh Bahadur Sahib, was also executed by Babar because he refused to convert to Islam. Just as it is said in the Gita, do not lament the death of a warrior for those who die in battle are honoured in heaven'.

But this was a memory he would have to live with all his life.

EPILOGUE

On 18 May 2009, the Sri Lankan Government announced that Prabhakaran had been killed while trying to escape the advancing Sri Lanka Army troops in the north of the country. The next day, his body was shown on Sri Lankan media, and a week later, Tamil Tiger spokesman Selvarasa Pathmanathan admitted that Prabhakaran had died on May 17.

The LTTE, under his leadership, had waged a sophisticated and highly potent guerrilla war against the GoSL. Fighting this war had left the country economically shattered, and the ripples of it will be felt for many decades to come. The elimination of Prabhakaran and the dissolution of the 'Tigers' is only an interregnum, and as the economic state of the island worsens, the Tiger will raise its head and wag its tail.

It is also well documented that the naked ambition of Gen K Sundarji, the then COAS, was disguised by his mesmerising personality, amply supported by his intellect. He had the politicians and the bureaucracy eating out of his hands. The most powerful aspect of Sundarji's personality was his charisma and his command of language. He was an impressive figure—dashing, slim, and dark-skinned, coupled with a flamboyance that would get him through to people who did not understand a word of what he said. His speech has traces of his Tamilian ancestry but his quick-wittedness always seemed to help him select the most effective words and phrases. He was also probably the most well-read man in the army at that point in time. It was mainly this aspect that had such a positive impact on political leadership.

It was during his tenure as the COAS that the Indian Army found itself committed to various operations and peacetime exercises that nearly brought the country to the brink of war with Pakistan. He definitely came into prominence after Op Bluestar and Woodrose, both of which were criticised for the excessive use of force and lack of intelligence. The Indian Army was involved in:

- Op Brasstacks which was the largest exercise ever taken on by the Indian Army

- Op Checkerboard I to III and Op Falcon against China
- The capture of the Quaid Post of the Pakistanis in Siachen Glacier, which was renamed Bana Post after the capture
- A covert and cynical winter offensive against Pakistan to capture POK
- Hurriedly committing IPKF in Sri Lanka without any intelligence and worse, without any higher directions of war. It was an overseas reach, which a third-world country could ill afford

13 Sikh LI completed its tenure and moved back to its earlier location, Gwalior, on 15 December 1989. In two years, the young unit had transformed into a battle-hardened fighting machine and is held in good stead even today.

Casualties

At the LZ on 12 Oct 1987: Killed Maj Birendra Singh, Sub Sampuran Singh, Havs Ajit Singh, Sawaran Singh, Kashmir Singh, LHav Sher Singh, Nks Mukhtiar Singh, Satwinder Singh, Surjit Singh, Gurmail Singh, L/Nks Manjit Singh, Darshan Singh, Seps Sukhwant Singh, Kulwant Singh, Kuldip Singh, Harjinder Singh, Gurnam Singh, Gurdial Singh, Ranjit Singh, Bakshish Singh, Somnath, Sakinder

Singh, Sukhwinder Singh, Gurbax Singh, Lal Singh, Jarnail Singh, Sohan Singh, Satnam Singh, and Joginder Singh. Total: One Offr, one JCO, and twenty-seven ORs

Main Body: Killed Maj US Ghosh, Sub Teja Singh, Nb Sub Darshan Singh, Hav Lachhman Singh, Nks Nirmal Singh, (292) Darshan Singh, Dalbir Singh, L/Nks Chamkaur Singh, Nath Singh, Dharam Singh, Seps Nahar Singh, Bhupinder Singh, Amrik Singh, Nirwail Singh, Bakhtaur Singh, Malkiat Singh, Satpal Singh, Balbir Singh, Darshan Singh, Balkar Singh, Gurjant Singh, Sep (Safai) Din Mohammed, and Mohan Gachhayat. Total: One Offr, two JCOs, and twenty ORs

Awards

The following awards were given for the op at the LZ on 12 October 1987:

- **Vir Chakras — 04**. Maj Birendra Singh (Posthumous), Sub Sampuran Singh (Posthumous), Sep Kuldip Singh, (Posthumous), and Sep Sukhwant Singh (Posthumous)
- **Sena Medals — 05**. Havs Ajit Singh (Posthumous), Sarvan Singh (Posthumous), Kashmir Singh (Posthumous), L/Hav Sher Singh (Posthumous), and (052) L/Nk Darshan Singh (Posthumous)

The unit won the following awards for ops in the Vavuniya Sector:

- **Yudh Seva Medal — 01**. Lt Col RS Sethi
- **Sena Medals — 03**. Maj US Ghosh (Posthumous), Maj Raghbir Singh, and Sub Teja Singh (Posthumous)
- **COAS Commendation — 01.** Nb Sub Ajit Singh

ABBREVIATIONS

10 Para Cdo – 10th Battalion of The Parachute Regiment (Commando)

13 Sikh LI – 13th Battalion of The Sikh Light Infantry Regiment

84 mm RL – 84 Millimetre Rocket launcher

Air Cmdr – Air Commodore

BFNA – Battlefield Nursing Assistants

Brig – Brigadier

Capt – Captain

CMG – Carbine Machine Gun

COAS – Chief of the Army Staff (Chief of Indian Army)

Col – Colonel

DZ – Dropping Zone (An area where airborne troops are dropped by parachute or slither down)

FIBUA – Fighting in Built-Up Areas

Flt Lt – Flight Lieutenant

GOC – General Officer Commanding

GOC-in-C – General Officer Commanding in Chief (Commander of an Army in this case Southern Army Commander)

GOSL – Government of Sri Lanka

Hav – Havildar

HE – High Explosive

Heptr – Helicopter

HMG – Heavy Machine Gun

HQs – Headquarters

IED – Improvised Explosive Device

IPKF – Indian Peace Keeping Force (In Sri Lanka)

LMG – Light Machine Gun

Lt Gen – Lieutenant General

LTTE – Liberation Tigers of Tamil Eelam

LZ – Landing Zone (An area where the aircraft lands and troops disembark)

Maj – Major

Maj Gen – Major General

OFC – Overall Force Commander (Of Troops in Sri Lanka)

Ops – Operations

R&AW – Research & Analysis Wing

RAP – Regimental Aid Post

RMO – Regimental Medical Officer (Doctor)

SLR – Self-loading Rifle

Sqn Ldr – Squadron Leader

Sub – Subedar

Tps – Troops

Wg Cdr/ Winco – Wing Commander